W9-BED-604

African-American Religion

Religion in American Life

JON BUTLER & HARRY S. STOUT
GENERAL EDITORS

African American-Religion

Albert J. Raboteau

OXFORD UNIVERSITY PRESS
New York • Oxford

To my children—Albert Jordy Raboteau III, Emily Ishem Raboteau, Charles David Raboteau, and Martin John Raboteau

Oxford University Press

Oxford New York
Athens Auckland Bangkok Bogotá Buenos Aires Calcutta
Cape Town Chennai Dar es Salaam Delhi Florence Hong Kong Istanbul
Karachi Kuala Lumpur Madrid Melbourne Mexico City Mumbai
Nairobi Paris São Paulo Singapore Taipei Tokyo Toronto Warsaw
and associated companies in
Berlin Ibadan

Library of Congress Cataloging-in-Publication Data

Raboteau, Albert J.
African-American religion/Albert J. Raboteau.
p. cm. — (Religion in American life)
Includes bibliographical references and index.
Summary: Examines the history of religious practice by African Americans and the
development of religious institutions, regional movements, and important
personalities from the time of slavery up to the twentieth century.
ISBN 0-19-510680-6
1. Afro-Americans—Religion—Juvenile literature. [1. Afro-Americans—
Religion.] I. Title. II. Series.
BR563.N4R235 1999   98-33669
277.3'0089'96073—dc21

9 8 7 6 5 4 3 2 1

Printed in the United States of America
on acid-free paper

Design and layout: Loraine Machlin
Picture research: Lisa Kirchner

On the cover: Martin Luther King, Mountain Top, *by Romare Bearden.*
 © Romare Bearden Foundation/Licensed by VAGA, New York, NY

Frontispiece: *Children attend a Roman Catholic Mass in Chicago in 1945.*

Contents

Introduction

JON BUTLER & HARRY S. STOUT, GENERAL EDITORS

The history of African-American religion exemplifies America's long and dramatic engagement with ethnic pluralism and the central role of race in shaping American life. Thousands of Africans from diverse cultures and religious traditions, forcibly transported to America as slaves, retained many African customs even as they converted to Christianity. Before and after the Civil War, African Americans drew religion to its moral and prophetic calling, making it the center not only of African-American culture but of a challenging ethic of equality and dignity throughout American society.

African-American Religion highlights all the excitement of the African-American religious experience in America. It reveals the powerful interweaving of traditional African religious themes with Christianity, the challenge of African-American religion to slavery, and the two-century quest for freedom that so often centered in African-American churches. From the African Methodist Episcopal Church to the Nation of Islam, from Richard Allen and Jarena Lee to Ida B. Wells and Martin Luther King, *African-American Religion* explains how personal sacrifice and inspired leadership created on of America's most powerful and distinctive religious institutions.

This book is part of a unique 17-volume series that explores the evolution, character, and dynamics of religion in American life from 1500 to the end of the 20th century. As late as the 1960s, historians paid relatively little attention to religion beyond studies of New England's Puritans. But since then, American religious history and its contemporary expression have been the subject of intense inquiry. These new studies have thoroughly transformed our knowledge of almost every American religious group and have fully revised our understanding of religion's role in American history.

It is impossible to capture the flavor and character of the American experience without understanding the connections between secular activities and religion. Spirituality stood at the center of Native American societies before European colonization and has continued to do so long after. Religion—and the freedom to express it—motivated millions of immigrants to come to America from remarkably different cultures, and the exposure to new ideas and ways of living shaped their experience. It also fueled tension among different ethnic and racial groups in America, and regrettably accounted for difficult episodes of bigotry in American society. Religion urged Americans to expand the nation—first within the continental United States, then through overseas conquests and missionary work—and has had a profound influence on American politics, from the era of the Puritans to the present. Finally, religion contributes to the extraordinary diversity that has, for four centuries, made the United States one of the world's most dynamic societies.

The Religion in American Life series explores the historical traditions that have made religious freedom and spiritual exploration central features of American society. It emphasizes the experience of religion in America—what men and women have understood by religion, how it has affected politics and society, and how Americans have used it to shape their daily lives.

Religion in American Life

JON BUTLER & HARRY S. STOUT
GENERAL EDITORS

Chapter 1

Beginnings

t was dawn when the villagers caught sight of the raiding party, 30 strong, landing on the shore. As people fled their huts in alarm, the invaders attacked, shouting "St. George" and "Santiago." Those people who were not killed or immediately captured sought desperately to escape. Some ran into the sea and drowned. Some tried to hide beneath their huts. Others attempted to conceal their children in the bushes. But it was no use; all were discovered and forced onto ships. A total of 165 men, women, and children were taken captive that day.

The ships lay at anchor while the raiders took more prisoners. Then they set sail, bearing their captives farther and farther from home; where they were going and why they were taken the prisoners did not know. When the ships landed, the whole lot, now more than 200, were taken ashore and assembled on a field outside the gates of a city. There the unusually large number of captives and the variety of their complexions—white, brown, and black—provided a novel spectacle for the crowd of onlookers who gathered from miles around.

Weakened by the voyage, disoriented, and frightened, the captives began to groan and weep; some cried aloud to God. Others struck their faces with their hands and threw themselves to the ground. Several sang the funeral songs of their homeland. Many became frantic as the captors began to divide the crowd into smaller groups, separating, in the process,

This bead-covered banner used in Haitian Vodou depicts St. Jacques, who in turn represents a warrior god of African origin. In Haiti, Catholic saints were identified with African gods.

A slave "coffle," or line of captives, marches to the African coast, where a ship will take them across the Atlantic Ocean into a life of slavery. The Atlantic slave trade brought millions of men, women, and children into slavery; many died on the way.

parents from children, husbands from wives, relatives from relatives, friends from friends. Children, dragged from parents, struggled free to run back to them; mothers shielded their children with their bodies and were beaten for hindering the separation; husbands clung desperately to wives. The sight of such misery moved some spectators unexpectedly to tears. Eventually, the partition completed, the captives came face to face with their fate—slavery for life.

Around the middle of the 15th century, Portuguese crusaders of the military Order of Christ (knights who promised to observe rules of poverty, chastity, and obedience) sailed down the coast of Africa in search of a new sea route to the Indies and direct access to the South Asian trade in spices and silks. They also planned to tap the major source of the gold that North African Muslim traders obtained south of the Sahara in "bilad as-Sudan," the land of the blacks. In addition, they hoped to contact a legendary Christian king, called Prester John, to persuade him to join them in their crusade against the followers of Islam. For centuries

Christians and Muslims had been fighting and enslaving each other around the borders of the Mediterranean Sea. Now the Portuguese were carrying the crusade into uncharted waters of the Atlantic Ocean.

In 1441, they attacked West African villages, shouting "St. George" and "Santiago" (St. James), the saints they always appealed to when raiding the outposts of Islam. The captives they took were enslaved as prisoners of what the Portuguese considered a just war. When raids became less successful, the Portuguese shifted to trading with coastal African peoples for gold, spices, and more slaves. Within 50 years Portugal had developed a seaborne trade in African slaves and established sugar production by slave labor on several island plantations—models that would soon be carried across the Atlantic Ocean. What these seafaring expeditions set in motion was the development of an expanding network of interlocking commercial, political, and cultural relations between diverse peoples by means of the Atlantic Ocean. The creation of a transatlantic world brought widely disparate peoples of Africa, Europe, and North and South America into contact, conflict, and cultural exchange.

Christopher Columbus's voyages in search of a western route to the Indies revealed to Europeans peoples and lands that they did not know existed. These discoveries of a "new world" quickly led Spain, Portugal's rival, to claim possession of vast areas of the Western Hemisphere. The Spanish depended on the labor of native peoples to turn the lands they conquered into profit-making colonies modeled on systems used successfully in Spain, Portugal, and the African Atlantic islands of Madeira and São Tomé. But warfare, overwork, and disease drastically reduced the native population, so the Spanish colonists began requesting the Crown to allow them to import African slaves (first from Spain and later directly from Africa) to solve their labor shortage. Among the people insisting that slave laborers replace Indians, the Dominican friar Bartolomé de las Casas became famous for defending the human rights of Native Americans. Las Casas presumed that the Africans had been taken captive in just wars. When he learned the actual circumstances of Atlantic slavery, he repented of his earlier requests, as he recounted in his *History of the Indies*:

> Before sugar mills were invented, some settlers, who had some wealth they had gotten from the sweat and blood of the Indians, wanted a license to buy black slaves back in Castile. The settlers saw they were killing off the Indians. . . . So they promised the cleric Bartolomé de las Casas that if he succeeded in getting them the license to import a dozen blacks to the island, they would allow the Indians they held to be set free. With this promise in mind, the cleric Las Casas got the king to allow the Spaniards of the islands to bring in some black slaves from Castile so the Indians could then be set free. . . . The cleric, many years later, regretted the advice he gave the king on this matter . . . when he saw proven that the enslavement of blacks was every bit as unjust as that of the Indians. It was not, in any case, a good solution he had proposed, that blacks be brought in so Indians could be freed. And this even though he thought that the blacks had been justly enslaved. He was not certain that his ignorance and his good intentions would excuse him before the judgment of God.

In 1502 the first shipment of African slaves reached the island of Hispaniola. As the Spanish, and then the Portuguese, the Dutch, the French, and the English established systems of slavery in their American colonies over the next century and a half, the Atlantic slave trade grew from a trickle to a flood. In the Mediterranean world, Africans had been one among many peoples trapped in slavery, but slavery in the Atlantic world took on a racial definition that identified slave status with Africans and the black color of their skin. Over the next three and a half centuries, approximately 10 to 12 million Africans survived the misery of the middle passage to toil in the mines, plantations, factories, and households of the Western Hemisphere. Until the 1830s more Africans than Europeans crossed the Atlantic. Then the percentage of European immigrants finally surpassed the percentage of Africans brought to the Americas in chains.

As a result of this massive movement of people, Africans contributed not only their labor, but also their culture, music, dance, language, art, and religion to the multiracial and multicultural societies that constituted in this sense a truly new world.

The Africans and the Europeans who crossed the Atlantic came from many different peoples. Their languages, cultures, and religions differed from people to people, even those within close distance of each other. The vast majority of American slaves came from West Africa, which extends

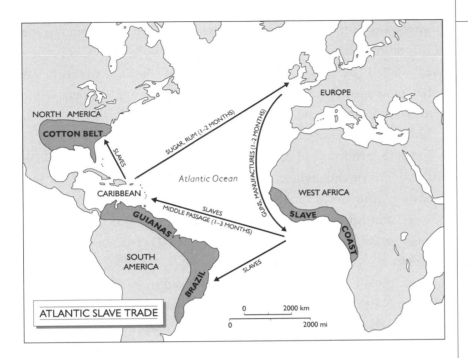

ATLANTIC SLAVE TRADE

The trade in slaves brought profits to slave traders in Europe, Africa, and the Americas. The trade in human "cargo" separated individual Africans from their homelands, families, and friends, and transported African culture across the Atlantic.

from the Senegambia region to the Bay of Benin, and from west central Africa, the area of Kongo-Angola (present-day Democratic Republic of the Congo and Angola). Different African peoples were drawn into the Atlantic trade at different times. For example, the Wolof and Serer, from the region between the Senegal and Gambia rivers, were enslaved from the start, whereas the Yoruba of modern-day Nigeria did not cross the Atlantic in significant numbers until the 19th century, and people of the Kongo came both early and late. In the American colonies Africans from different groups were thrown into contact with each other. Indeed, it was only after they were brought to the Americas that Africans began to think of themselves as just Africans, instead of Ibo, Akan, or Bakongo. Slavery itself, which mixed Africans from various regions, tended, on the one hand, to emphasize the separateness of the slaves' origins, and on the other to emphasize the areas of similarity that made communication and cooperation among them possible.

No less than language, music, and art, the religion of Africans showed a wide range of diversity. Islam, extended from North Africa by way of trans-Saharan trade routes, reached the Sudan and beyond by the 11th century. The Senegambia region, where the Wolof and other peoples had adopted Islam, supplied a large number of Muslim Africans to the Atlantic slave trade. Christianity had entered Egypt and Ethiopia in the 3rd and 4th centuries and inspired the growth of desert monasteries in which monks and nuns lived apart from society, practicing the virtues of obedience, poverty, and celibacy. The teaching and example of these African "fathers and mothers of the desert," as they came to be called, had a lasting influence on monasticism as it spread to Western Europe, Greece, and Russia. Christianity in Atlantic Africa was carried to the Kongo by the Portuguese in the 16th century. There the ruler, Nzinga Mvemba, accepted Christian baptism in 1506.

Africans, both free and slave, had arrived in Portugal and Spain through North Africa since the early Middle Ages. Many had learned the Europeans' languages and had accepted their religion. Reflecting their status as baptized Christians, they were called *ladinos* (literally "latins," meaning Spanish or Portuguese speakers). In fact the first Africans in the Americas—some arrived as free people, some as slaves—were *ladinos*. Because *ladino* slaves developed a reputation for running away and encouraging Indians to rebel, Spanish authorities on Hispaniola request- ed that they be prohibited and that *bozales* (unbaptized, "uncivilized") slaves be sent instead. Although Muslim and Christian Africans were swept up in the Atlantic slave trade, the vast majority of those enslaved in the Americas practiced the traditional religions of their ancestors.

African societies maintained ancient religious traditions that explained the nature of the world and the meaning of human existence. In addition to explaining reality, religion provided Africans with rituals to celebrate important events in life, such as birth, coming of age, marriage, and death. By means of their rituals, Africans also attempted to predict and to control misfortunes such as disease, flood, illness, or drought. They believed that God created the universe and everything in it. Many African peoples also believed that there were additional supernatural spirits (some of them ancestors) who acted in the daily lives of human beings to protect them from harm. If people lived good lives and honored the spirits and ancestors by prayer and sacrifice, all would be well. If people did evil, however, or neglected the spirits, they not only lost the spirits' protection, they risked arousing their anger. Spirits, though invisible, took form in human mediums, as well as in masks, medicines, and material containers that gave people physical access to their spiritual power. Ritual brought human beings and spirits into direct contact through ceremonial drumming, singing, and dancing, which moved priests and worshipers to enter into trancelike states in which they acted and spoke as the spirits themselves.

Europeans who entered the world of the Atlantic also came from many different peoples and nations: Spain, Portugal, the Netherlands, France, Denmark, and Britain. Christianity, the predominant religion of Europeans, differed significantly from place to place. In the early 16th century, as the Spanish were establishing colonies in the Americas, the Protestant Reformation broke European Christianity into two major branches, Catholic and Protestant, with lots of regional and national differences subdividing these as well.

European Christians, like Africans, believed that God created the world and sustained everything in it, although they preached that the one God existed in three divine persons, the Father, the Son, and the Holy Spirit. Catholic Europeans also directed prayers to holy ancestors called saints. Unlike Africans, they did not think the saints were divine, but they did believe the saints had miraculous powers to help the living, especially in time of need. Saints (like St. George, patron of Portugal, and St. James, called "the moorslayer" because of his status as the patron of crusaders fighting the Muslims) were expected to appeal to God on behalf of their clients and to act themselves when called upon to protect the faithful from harm. Like Africans, Catholic Europeans made special offerings to the saints and dedicated special days to celebrate stories of their miraculous deeds. The saints dwelled in an invisible place

A 16th-century carving of Santiago (St. James), the patron saint of the Portuguese and the Spanish in their wars against the Muslims. Africans enslaved in the Americas identified Santiago with the warrior god Ogun.

called heaven but made themselves available to the faithful on Earth in statues, pictures, medals, and relics that had been charged, by a priest's blessing, to convey their spiritual power.

With few exceptions, European and European-American Christians believed that they were justified in conquering American Indians and enslaving Africans to spread the religions and cultures of Europe, which they assumed were superior to those of other peoples. Church and state officials issued orders to colonists in America to arrange for the religious instruction of slaves. In the Catholic colonies of Spain, Portugal, and France, members of religious orders (communities specially dedicated to lives of prayer, poverty, celibacy, and obedience), such as the Franciscans, the Dominicans, the Jesuits, and the Ursulines, undertook the task. But they faced many obstacles, including opposition from slave owners, lack of interest on the part of slaves, and the practical difficulties of language, time, and access involved in trying to teach slaves bound to long hours of exhausting work. Occasionally special classes were held to teach slaves the basic doctrines of Christianity. Over time, some slaves did become Christian. But this did not mean that they abandoned the religious beliefs and practices of Africa. Catholic slaves continued to observe African religious customs, such as venerating ancestors and praying to African spirits.

In effect they chose to have two paths to access spiritual power, just as European Christians continued to observe pre-Christian religious customs (often identified as magic or superstition by religious authorities). For example, many people wore charms to ward off "the evil eye" or invested special places and physical objects with spiritual power long after Christianity had spread to Europe—and some continue to do this even today. Worried that slaves were mixing African rituals, such as offering sacrifices to the gods, with Catholicism, colonial church officials brought them to trial before church courts on charges of witchcraft and magic. In 1722, for example, a Catholic priest complained that the slaves in Haiti "secretly preserve all the superstition of their ancient idolatrous cult alongside the ceremonies of Christianity"; and in 1792 a meeting of Haitian clergymen noted that supposedly Christian slaves continued to mingle "the Holy utensils of our religion with profane and idolatrous objects."

Confraternities (religious societies) organized the religious activities of slaves and free blacks, requiring their members to practice the moral code of Catholicism, to assist one another in time of need, and to observe the major ceremonial days of the church's calendar, especially the days dedicated to the saint in whose honor the confraternity was named. The largest black confraternity was dedicated to Our Lady of the Holy Rosary and included black Catholics in Portugal, Spain, Brazil, Peru, and Kongo. On major religious holidays black and white confraternities marched in colorful processions, with music, costumes, and flags representing each group. By encouraging blacks, as well as whites, to join confraternities, the clergy hoped to increase their devotion to religious practice. The confraternities also enabled the slaves to organize their own religious communities and customs. The black confraternities in Peru, Cuba, and Brazil admitted their members according to the specific region of their African origins, such as Dahomey or Kongo-Angola.

In the American colonies established by Catholic Europeans from Spain, Portugal, or France, Africans observed the importance of the saints in Catholic piety and identified them with African gods and spirits who shared similar powers, characteristics, or areas of influence. In Brazil and Cuba, for example, the Virgin Mary, depicted in robes of white and blue and holding the child Jesus, resembled Yemanja, a god of the Yoruba people of present-day Nigeria, whose favorite colors were blue and white and who was honored as the patron of childbirth. Making creative use of the similarities between Catholicism and the religions of Africa, African slaves and their African-American descendents incorporated elements from Catholicism and from diverse African religions into new African-American religions. In Brazil these African-influenced religious communities came to be called Candomblê, in Cuba they were named Santería, and in Haiti, Vodou (sometimes spelled "voodoo").

While these religions incorporated Catholic and, to a lesser degree, Indian influences, they maintained a predominantly African character in theological beliefs and in ritual practice. Although African gods were identified with Catholic saints, it was the stories about the African gods that were preserved in the teachings and rituals of the Candomblê, Santería,

Practitioners of Vodou leave offerings and pay homage to the Vodou queen Marie Leveau at her grave in St. Louis Cemetery No. 1 in New Orleans. Leveau, born the daughter of plantation owner and a slave in the 1790s and raised a Roman Catholic, was renowned for her supernatural powers.

and Vodou communities. Similarly, African styles of worship, focused on dancing, drumming, and spiritual trances, predominated in their services. In Brazil and Cuba, the memberships of the confraternities and those of the Candomblé and Santería communities sometimes overlapped.

Precisely because of their adaptability, African religions could embrace new gods and new rituals without losing their fundamental character. It was their ability to change that allowed them to maintain continuity with Africa in the slave societies of America. The African spirits, called *lwa* in Haiti and *santos* in Cuba, might take on new identities across the Atlantic, or new spirits might be revealed. But the spirits were still served in accordance with the age-old African ways.

In ceremonies of worship and communion, drummers played the distinctive rhythms that belonged to each of the gods, beckoning them from their home in "Guinen" (Guinea) to join in celebration with their servants across the sea. Directed by the priest or priestess, the community gathered to sing and dance the praises of the spirits who had power to grant their wishes and to keep them safe from harm. The *lwa* and *santos,* represented by entranced priests and people, solved individual and community problems and offered instruction about things that needed to be done. Altars, covered with images of the saints, enabled the congregation to offer food and drink to please their gods. Priests also sacrificed animals to the spirits because blood contained the power of life that strengthened the *lwa* and the *santos.* Then the congregation cooked and ate the animals' flesh in a service of communion that gave the people assembled a share in the spirits' power. Each member of the Vodou or Santería community had a special patron spirit, a relationship established by initiation ceremonies which, in some cases, "wedded" a person and a spirit together in a life of mutual responsibility and care.

As the driving rhythm of the drums, the singing, and the dancing, all choreographed to traditional African patterns, mounted in intensity and excitement, the slaves experienced an intimate relationship with the gods that enriched their lives and left them feeling renewed.

Protestant Europeans, like Catholics, claimed that the potential conversion of slaves to Christianity justified the enslavement of Africans. But British Americans resisted religious instruction of their slaves because they suspected that it was illegal under British law to hold a fellow Christian in bondage. If this were true, baptizing a slave would in effect free him, contrary to the slaveowner's economic interest. Colonial legislators solved the problem by passing decrees that baptism had no effect upon the status of the baptized in regard to slavery or freedom. Despite the legislation, British American slaveholders remained suspicious of teaching Christianity to slaves because they believed that becoming Christian would raise the slaves' self-esteem, persuade them that they were equal to whites, and encourage them to become rebellious. Religious assemblies might present slaves with the opportunity to organize

resistance, and teaching slaves to read the Bible would have the dangerous effect of making them literate.

British-American Protestants also feared that including Africans in the fellowship of Christian community would blur the cultural and social distinctions that an effective system of slavery required. Although the colonists resisted, the English church and government authorities repeatedly encouraged them to obey their duty to instruct their slaves in the Christian faith. Concerned that Protestants seemed less devoted to missions than Catholics, the English bishops challenged the Protestant colonists to live up to the example of the Catholic missions in converting the Indians and the African slaves.

An overseas missionary society, the Society for the Propagation of the Gospel in Foreign Parts (SPG), supported English clergymen to work among slaves, Indians, and white settlers in the English colonies. Founded in London in 1701, the SPG circulated pamphlets stressing the value of Christian instruction for slaves. Christianity, the society's officers argued, would not inspire rebellion among the slaves. On the contrary, they argued in sermons, letters, and pamphlets, the Bible itself supported the slave system. Quoting St. Paul's Epistle to the Ephesians, 6:1, "Slaves be obedient to your masters," and other biblical texts, they tried to overcome the suspicions of masters by presenting Christianity as a system of slave control.

The success of missions to the slaves depended on circumstances beyond the missionaries' control: the proportion of African-born to American-born slaves, the geographic location and work patterns of the slaves, and the ratio of blacks to whites in a particular area. Missionaries had little success with African-born slaves, because many of them never learned English well enough to understand instruction in Christianity. American-born slaves, who understood the language and the customs of the whites, made better candidates for conversion. The frequency of contact between blacks and whites also affected the chances of succesful instruction of the slaves. Blacks in the north and in the Chesapeake Bay region of Maryland and Virginia, for example, had closer contact with

whites than did those of the low-lying coastal areas of South Carolina and Georgia, where large gangs of African slaves worked on isolated rice and cotton plantations with only limited exposure to whites or their religion.

Even if a missionary gained regular access to slaves, the slaves did not always accept the Christian message. Some rejected it precisely because it was the religion of those who held them in bondage. Others accepted Christianity because they hoped—contrary to colonial legislation and missionary preaching—that baptism would raise their status and lead eventually to freedom for their children, if not for themselves. The Reverend Francis Le Jau, an Anglican missionary in South Carolina, found it necessary to require slaves to take the following oath before he would baptize them:

> You declare in the presence of God and before this Congregation that you do not ask for the holy baptism out of any design to free yourself from the Duty and Obedience that you owe to your Master while you live, but merely for the good of Your Soul and to partake of the Graces and Blessings promised to the members of the Church of Jesus Christ.

Colonial clergy had established a few successful missions among the slaves by the early 18th century, but these successes were dwarfed by the enormous size and difficulty of the task. When the bishop of London distributed a list of questions in 1724 asking ministers to describe their work among the slaves, several reported impressive numbers of baptisms. The majority, however, mentioned goals and intentions instead of concrete achievements. The very method of religious instruction, as conceived by

Two Catholic slaves of African descent pray the rosary in Peru before an image of the Virgin of Guadelupe. Africans accompanied the Spanish conquistadors into Mexico and Peru in the early 16th century.

colonial Anglicans, made it difficult to convert adult slaves. Becoming Christian involved a lengthy process of learning, memorization, and moral testing. During the first 120 years of black slavery in British North America, little headway was made in converting the slave population to Christianity.

The conversion of slaves in large numbers was a product of a period of religious revivals that swept parts of the colonies beginning in 1739. These extended meetings of prayer and preaching stirred intense religious emotion among crowds of people and led many to experience conversion. Leaders of the revivals made special mention of the fact that blacks attended their gatherings in larger numbers than seen before. Some were allowed to attend by their masters; others risked punishment to attend without permission. Not only did free blacks and slaves attend revivals, they also took active part in the services, praying, exhorting, and preaching. Revivals succeeded where earlier efforts failed for a number of reasons. The missionaries and pastors of the Anglican church had depended upon a slow process of memorization and education to instruct the slaves in Christianity. The revivalist preachers emphasized the immediate experience of conversion as the primary requirement for baptism and so made becoming Christian a less time-consuming and difficult process. Because of their concentration on the experience of conversion, the revival preachers tended to downplay learning, wealth, or status as requirements for religious leadership. All classes of society were welcome to participate actively in prayer meetings and revival services in which the poor, the illiterate, and even the enslaved were permitted to preach and pray in public.

In addition to the revivals, the American Revolution in the last quarter of the 18th century called into question the legitimacy of slavery. The justness of the revolutionary cause was based upon the natural rights of the American colonists to liberty. Slaves quickly pointed out the discrepancy between the colonists' struggle for liberty from British oppression and the colonists' oppression of Africans held in slavery.

At the start of the Revolution, slaves issued a series of petitions for freedom. A 1777 petition in Massachusetts noted that the black petitioners

"Cannot but express their Astonishment that It has Never Bin Considered that Every Principle from which Amarica has Acted in the Cours of their unhappy Deficultes with Great Briton Pleads Stronger than A thousand arguments in favour of your petioners . . . [who] ask" to be "restored to the enjoyments of that which is the Naturel Right of all men. . . . so may the Inhabitance of thes Stats No longer chargeable with the inconstancey of acting themselves the art which thay condem and oppose in others Be prospered in their present Glorious struggle for Liberty and have those Blessing to them . . ." The government of the colony ignored this and several more petitions like it. Although the Revolution did lead to the gradual abolition of slavery in the Northern states, in the South, where the vast majority of African Americans lived, slavery would still be the condition of their children's children.

After the Revolution, revivals continued to occur in the South and increasing numbers of slaves were moved to convert by the dramatic preaching of the revivalist ministers, especially Methodists and Baptists. The emotional excitement of the revivals encouraged those who attended to express their religious feelings. The sight of black and white converts weeping, shouting, fainting, and dancing in ecstatic trances became a familiar feature of the camp meeting revivals—outdoor gatherings for prayer and preaching that attracted large crowds and lasted from several days to a week. In this emotionally charged atmosphere, slaves encountered a form of Protestant worship that resembled the religious celebrations of their African homelands. The similarity between African and revival styles of worship made Christianity seem more familiar to the slaves and helped them to make sense of this new religion in terms of their old ones.

The growth of the Baptist and Methodist denominations, which accompanied the late 18th-century religious revivals, seemed for a time to challenge the system of slavery. An anti-Baptist petition warned the Virginia Assembly in 1777 that "there have been nightly meetings of slaves to receive the instruction of these teachers without the consent of their masters, which have produced very bad consequences." In 1780,

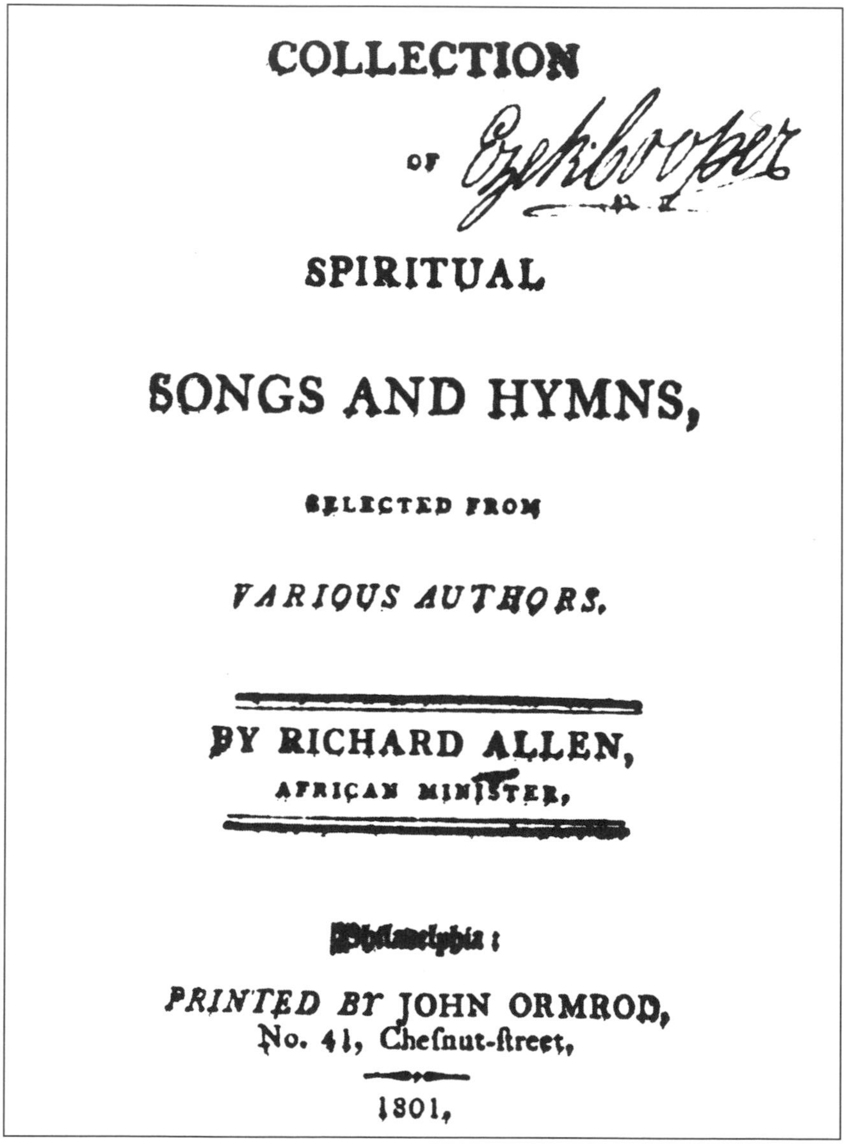

The spirituals and hymns that were sung at camp meetings and revivals at the end of the 18th century were collected and published by Richard Allen, founder of the AME church.

COLLECTION

OF *Ezekbooper*

SPIRITUAL

SONGS AND HYMNS,

SELECTED FROM

VARIOUS AUTHORS.

BY RICHARD ALLEN,
AFRICAN MINISTER,

Philadelphia:

PRINTED BY JOHN ORMROD,
No. 41, Chefnut-ftreet,

1801,

1783, and 1784, Methodist General Conferences of clergy and lay leaders strongly condemned slavery and passed regulations prohibiting ministers, and then the membership as a whole, from owning, buying, and selling slaves. Several Baptist leaders freed their slaves, and in 1789 the General Committee of Virginia Baptists condemned slavery as a "violent deprivation of the rights of nature."

In the South, these antislavery moves met quick opposition. As a result, the Methodist Conference suspended its rules against slavery in 1785. Local Baptist groups in Virginia declared that the issue of slavery was a matter best left to each individual's conscience. The majority of both groups decided that the immediate goal of the church should be to seek better treatment for the slaves, not their emancipation. Although both Methodists and Baptists rapidly retreated from their antislavery positions, their uneasiness about slavery initially gave slaves the impression that they were "friendly toward freedom," which helped increase the number of black converts attracted to these denominations.

Because Baptists and Methodists were willing to license black men to preach, a significant group of black preachers, free and slave, began during the 1770s and 1780s to pastor their own people. These pioneering black preachers were extremely important for the development of African-American Christianity. They applied the teachings of Christianity to the experience of the slaves (and free blacks) by interpreting the stories, symbols, and events of the Bible to fit the day-to-day lives of black people. Forming Christian communities among slaves and free blacks, these early black pastors began to build an independent black church in the last quarter of the 18th century. Slave preachers instructed their fellow slaves and led them to conversion, in some cases without the active involvement of white clergymen or masters at all. The growth of Baptist and Methodist churches between 1770 and 1820 changed the religious complexion of the South by bringing large numbers of slaves into membership in the church and by introducing even more to the basics of Christian belief and practice. The black church had been born.

Chapter 2

The Independent African Church Movement

The Baptist and Methodist challenge to slavery at the end of the 18th century failed, but revivalism did make it possible for African Americans to take for themselves a significant arena of freedom by licensing black men to preach and allowing them to establish separate black churches. Several "African" churches, as they were called, developed before 1800, some in spite of persecution. In the early 1780s, for example, a slave named Andrew Bryan began to preach and gathered a small group for worship outside the city of Savannah, Georgia. White citizens, worried about slave rebellion, had Andrew Bryan, his brother Sampson, and several others arrested and whipped twice for holding illegal meetings. According to an early Baptist historian, Andrew "told his persecutors that he rejoiced not only to be whipped, but *would freely suffer death for the cause of Jesus Christ.*" Eventually, local officials examined and released them with permission to continue their worship services, but only during daylight hours.

By 1790 Bryan's congregation had grown to a membership of 225 communicants and about 350 converts not yet admitted to full membership. The congregation became the First African Baptist Church of Savannah. In 1803, a Second African Church was organized from members of the First, and a few years later a Third African Church was formed, both led by black pastors. These churches were independent insofar as they met separately and chose their own ministers and officers.

Christian slaves in America sometimes worshiped with the family of their masters. They also met on their own to hold services without white supervision.

In the late 18th century, a group of pioneer black preachers began to convert their own people and founded separate black churches for worship. Andrew Bryan, a slave, formed an African Baptist Church in Savannah, Georgia, in 1790.

The independence of black churches and black ministers in the South was always threatened by restrictions, especially in reaction to reports of actual or rumored slave revolts, when all gatherings of blacks for whatever purpose were viewed with alarm. For slaves to participate in the organization, leadership, and conduct of churches seemed dangerous. Nevertheless, unlikely as it may seem, black churches continued to grow in the slaveholding South. Though by law they were supposed to be supervised by whites, some separate black congregations were in fact led by black preachers, slave and free. These separate black congregations were exceptions to the usual pattern in which slaves attended church with their masters, seated separately in balconies or back pews, or attended services at their home plantations and farms, presided over by a visiting white preacher.

In the North, the gradual abolition of slavery after the Revolution made it possible for black congregations and clergy to take much more authority over their religious affairs. And the separation of church and state decreed by the U.S. Constitution and successive state constitutions meant that no one denomination received official recognition by the government. By law, citizens had freedom of religious choice, and different denominations could compete on an equal basis for church members. In the first decades of the 19th century, church organization flourished—among blacks as well as whites. Between 1790 and 1820, black Episcopalians, Methodists, Baptists, and Presbyterians founded churches and struggled with church leaders to exercise varying degrees of independence from white control.

Among the first to do so was Bethel African Methodist Episcopal Church in Philadelphia, founded in 1794 by Richard Allen, a former slave and Methodist preacher. Bethel was organized after an incident of racial discrimination drove many of the black members out of St. George's, the church they had supported for years. One Sunday morning in the early 1790s, the black members of St. George's learned to their surprise that they could not sit in the benches they normally used. Instead, they were ordered to sit upstairs in a balcony that had recently been added at the rear of the church. Although the situation was unfair—like the whites, they had contributed to the remodeling of the church—they obeyed the order. As the opening prayer began, one of the white ushers told Absalom Jones, a respected black parishioner, to get up and move from the front to the back of the balcony. Jones, a dignified man in his late 40s, asked the usher to wait until prayer ended, but the white man insisted he move immediately and motioned for another usher to help him lift Jones from his knees. As soon as the prayer was over, Jones and the rest of the black worshipers stood and walked out of the church in a body.

This incident, described years later in Allen's *Life and Gospel Labors,* was being commemorated in annual sermons and children's pageants a century later as the founding event of black Methodism and black religious independence. Even though Allen and a committee of black Methodists built Bethel Church with their own funds, the local Methodist authorities claimed ownership of the church property. When white Methodist ministers demanded control, Allen and his congregation refused and fought the case all the way to the Pennsylvania Supreme Court, which decided in their favor. Similar conflicts with white Methodists elsewhere convinced black Methodists to send delegates to a conference in Philadelphia to discuss their common problems. Meeting at Bethel Church in 1816, they formed the African Methodist Episcopal Church and elected Richard Allen as its bishop. Two other denominations of black Methodists were formed around the same time: the Union Church of Africans, led by Peter Spencer in Wilmington, Delaware, in 1815, and the African Methodist Episcopal Zion Church (called "Zion" to distinguish it from Allen's group), established in New York City in 1821.

Though the black Methodists were the first to take independent control of their church property, finances, and government on the denominational level, blacks in other churches in the North demonstrated a spirit of independence as well. St. Thomas African Episcopal Church was founded in Philadelphia in 1794, and Absalom Jones was chosen as pastor and ordained a priest 10 years later. In 1804, an African Baptist Church was formed in Boston under the ministry of Thomas Paul. Paul also helped organize the Abyssinian Baptist Church of New York in 1808, which then called Josiah Bishop to be its minister. Bishop, a former slave, had

The African Episcopal Church of St. Thomas, founded in 1784, was the first black Episcopal Church in the United States. Under the leadership of Absalom Jones it grew to nearly 500 members within a few years.

previously served an interracial church in Portsmouth, Virginia, whose members purchased his freedom. The first African Presbyterian Church, established in Philadelphia in 1807, was led by John Gloucester, a former slave converted by a white Presbyterian who freed him and urged him to preach. These black churches formed the institutional structure for the development of free black communities. They also gave African Americans a platform to express publicly their own visions of Christianity and of the United States.

The main public issues that absorbed the attention of free blacks in the North were the social conditions of poverty and illiteracy that afflicted the majority of African-American communities, the continuation and expansion of slavery in the South, the legal and social discrimination that restricted the rights of free blacks, and coming to terms with the troubling existential question, what did the black experience in America mean? As the single institution that black communities controlled, churches played an active role in addressing these issues, as did their ministers through sermons, speeches, and deeds.

Black churches helped form self-help organizations, such as benevolent societies, that were designed to aid widows, to pay for burial of the poor, and to teach children to read and write. Moral reform societies also served to foster racial pride and community activism. Through these societies black people acted cooperatively to change the conditions in which they lived. Convinced that progress for the race and escape from poverty depended upon education, temperance (abstaining from the consumption of alcohol), thrift, and responsibility, black ministers emphasized the importance of moral behavior and self-respect.

Moreover, they were well aware that the cause of antislavery was linked to the moral respectability of the free black communities. One of the major arguments in defense of slavery stated that black people were inferior to whites and incapable of managing the responsibilities of free citizens. According to this racist view, blacks needed the discipline of slavery to control their laziness, ignorance, and immorality. Moral behavior, then, became all the more important to free blacks as proof of their equality to white people and their ability to succeed when given the same opportunity as whites to work and to educate their children. Black ministers such as Allen and Jones urged their congregations to practice the virtues of thrift, temperance, honesty, and hard work, not only to better their economic condition but also to disprove the prejudice that supported the system of slavery. While abuse of alcohol was a widespread problem in the early 19th century among whites as well as blacks, temperance became a racial, as well as moral, issue for blacks because incidents of drunkenness among blacks were used by supporters of slavery to argue that black people could not be responsible citizens.

Black churches defended the antislavery position that most white churches had abandoned or never held in the first place. They taught that slavery was incompatible with Christianity and any nation that permitted the sin of slavery risked divine punishment. When some of the most prominent white citizens of the nation founded the American Colonization Society in 1817 to support the emigration of free blacks from the United States to Africa, black leaders became concerned. They feared that the Colonization Society would pressure Congress into legislating the emigration of all free blacks and so rid the country of the most outspoken opponents of slavery. They did not object to the voluntary emigration of African Americans to Africa, but protested the view that free blacks had no place in the United States. In newspaper columns and speeches, they maintained that generations of black people had contributed their labor, sweat, and blood to the formation of this nation and, as much as anyone else, belonged there, in the country of their birth. Peter Williams, the pastor of St. Philip's Episcopal Church in New York, expressed the anticolonization argument in a speech he delivered on July 4, 1830:

> We are natives of this country, we ask only to be treated as well as foreigners. Not a few of our fathers suffered and bled to purchase its independence; we ask only to be treated as well as those who fought against it. We have toiled to cultivate it, and to raise it to its present prosperous condition; we ask only to share equal privileges with those who come from distant lands to enjoy the fruits of our labour. Let these moderate requests be granted, and we need not go to Africa nor anywhere else, to be improved and happy. We cannot but doubt the purity of the motives of those persons who deny us these requests, and would send us to Africa to gain what they might give us at home.

Without the activism of free black communities in the North, the antislavery movement would have been weakened. Continually reminded of slavery by family ties to the South and by the presence of fugitive slaves among them, free blacks (many of whom were former slaves themselves) joined antislavery societies and took action by offering sanctuary to runaway slaves. Many leaders of the antislavery movement were ministers. For example, a Committee of Vigilance, formed in New York by clergymen Christopher Rush, Theodore Wright, and Henry Highland Garnet, aided fugitive slaves on their way to freedom. Richard Allen and his wife, Sarah, sheltered fugitives in their Philadelphia home, and the basement of Bethel Church also furnished a safe stop for travelers on the Underground Railroad.

The Underground Railroad was a network of people who hid fugitive slaves and helped them escape to freedom in the Northern states and Canada. These antislavery activists operated a series of "stations" (safe hiding places) where escaping slaves could find shelter, food, and guidance on their difficult and dangerous journey north. Because slaves by law were considered the property of their owners, it was illegal to help them escape. Therefore, the "conductors," as supporters of the escaping slaves were called, depended upon secrecy (thus the name "underground") to keep the system working. Harriet Tubman, one of the most active agents of the Underground Railroad, had escaped to Canada from a slave plantation in Maryland in 1849. Despite the risk of capture and re-enslavement, she returned South 19 times to lead more than 300 slaves to freedom.

Fugitive slaves had to overcome difficult odds to make good their escape. They had to outrun or evade their masters or slave catchers; they had to find their way north through unfamiliar territory; and they had to guard constantly against the danger that someone might discover them and turn them over to law officers. If caught and returned to slavery, they might be severely whipped, placed in chains, or sold away from friends and family. Accounts of the experiences of fugitive slaves, published in the 1840s and 1850s, depicted scenes of dramatic chases, narrow escapes, and daring rescues. Some of the fugitive slave accounts romanticized the details, but the difficulties of escape were real, as was the overwhelming desire for freedom that inspired the slaves' dangerous flight.

THE

ANTI-SLAVERY RECORD.

VOL. III. No. VII. JULY, 1837. WHOLE No. 31.

This picture of a poor fugitive is from one of the stereotype cuts manufactured in this city for the southern market, and used on handbills offering rewards for runaway slaves.

Fugitive slaves were aided and supported by a network of black and white antislavery activists, who constituted an "underground railroad." Black churches and clergy played an active role in helping these runaways.

Once slaves had made it to a Northern state, they still lived in fear of recapture. Those who helped them also faced the possibility of arrest. Leonard Grimes, a black minister in Boston, for example, served a jail term for assisting slaves to escape. Black clergy, like Grimes, took a leadership role in the organization and growth of the abolitionist movement in the North. Eight black ministers were among the founders of the American and Foreign Anti-Slavery Society in 1840: Jehiel Beman, Amos Gerry Beman, Christopher Rush, Samuel Cornish, Theodore Wright, Stephen Gloucester (the son of early Philadelphia preacher John Gloucester), Henry Highland Garnet, and Andrew Harris.

Black clergymen also spoke out in favor of temperance and other moral reforms of the day. George Hogarth, an African Methodist Episcopal minister in Brooklyn, New York, combined the multifaceted roles of the active black minister by serving as a local supporter and informant for the antislavery newspaper *The Liberator,* edited in Boston by white abolitionist William Lloyd Garrison; organizing local opposition to the American Colonization Society; and starting a temperance association for people of color in 1831. These and other black ministers used the press, their pulpits, and public halls to debate, discuss, protest, and attempt to solve the deep problems confronting their communities.

One of the most effective written protests of the time, David Walker's *Appeal to the Coloured Citizens of the World,* was published in 1829. Walker was born free in North Carolina in 1785. He traveled North and settled in Boston, where he started a used-clothing shop in 1827. Self-taught, he spent his free time reading and studying. After publishing his *Appeal,* Walker made sure it got smuggled into the slaveholding states by giving it to sailors and by sewing copies into the pockets of the used clothing he sold. When copies of Walker's pamphlet were found circulating in the South, the governor of Georgia wrote to the mayor of Boston, demanding that he prohibit the publication of the *Appeal* and confiscate all published copies of the pamphlet. The mayor refused.

Walker's *Appeal* used religious and political arguments to convict the nation of criminal injustice because it allowed slavery to continue.

Warning of divine punishment, Walker reminded his readers that "God rules in the armies of heaven and among the inhabitants of the earth, having His ears continually open to the tears and groans of His oppressed people, and being . . . just and holy . . . will . . . one day appear fully in behalf of the oppressed, and arrest the progress of the avaricious." The history of civilization and the Bible proved that God overthrows oppressors by causing "them to rise up one against another, to be split and divided . . . to oppress each other, and . . . to open hostility with sword in hand." (In light of the ongoing dispute between North and South that would result in the Civil War, the *Appeal* seems prophetic.) Walker also criticized European-American Christianity by predicting that "if ever the world becomes Christianized . . . it will be through the means, under God of the *Blacks*, who are now held in wretchedness, and degradation by the white *Christians* of the world."

Protest eventually led to political organization—and again the church played a central role. An increase in the number of laws discriminating against blacks led black leaders to believe that they needed to form some national movement to fight for their rights. In response, the first of a series of national Negro conventions met in 1830 at Bethel Church in Philadelphia with Bishop Richard Allen acting as chair. There, the 40 delegates discussed the discrimination and poverty that confronted black citizens at every turn, and proceeded to organize the American Society of Free Persons of Colour, whose purpose was to improve conditions for black people in the United States and to establish a settlement in Canada for those driven from their homes by anti-black laws. In addition, the convention issued an address to free people of color, urging them to "pursue all legal means for the speedy elevation of ourselves and brethren to the scale and standing of men."

The convention met annually for six years and then continued irregularly until 1893. In 1843 the convention, meeting in Buffalo, New York, listened to an unusually powerful attack on slavery composed by one of the delegates, Henry Highland Garnet. Addressing the slaves themselves, Garnet declared: "To such degradation it is sinful in the extreme for you

Henry Highland Garnet—
clergyman, abolitionist,
and newspaper editor—
gave a fiery address at the
National Negro Conven-
tion in Buffalo, New York,
in 1843, urging slaves to
overthrow slavery through
active resistance.

to make voluntary submission . . . Neither God, nor Angels, or just men, command you to suffer for a single moment. . . . Therefore it is your solemn and imperative duty to use every means, both moral, intellectual, and physical, that promises success. . . . Brethren, arise! Strike for your lives and liberties. Now is the day and the hour. Let every slave throughout the land do this, and the days of slavery are numbered. You cannot be more oppressed than you have been—you cannot suffer greater cruelties than you have already. Rather die freemen than live to be slaves . . . Let your motto be resistance! Resistance! Resistance!"

Garnet himself had been born into slavery in 1815, in the state of Maryland. When Garnet was nine years old, his family and seven other slaves escaped North traveling by wagon and on foot. They settled first in New Hope, Pennsylvania, and a few years later moved to New York City. At the age of 11, Garnet enrolled in the African Free School on Mulberry Street. He later found work as a cook and steward on a schooner. After one voyage, he returned home to find his family scattered by slave catchers.

In 1835 he was admitted to an interracial school in Canaan, New Hampshire. Local whites attacked the school on July 4, using oxen to drag the school building into a swamp. Garnet organized black and white students to resist, and when night riders (a band of horsemen using the cover of darkness to terrorize and to hide their identities) appeared, the young man was one of the first to fire on them with a gun. In 1840 he graduated with honors from Oneida Institute, a four-year interracial college in upstate New York, and settled in Troy, New York. There he taught in a black school and edited a weekly newspaper, *The Clarion*.

In 1843 he was ordained a Presbyterian minister and appointed pastor of Troy's Liberty Street Church. That same year he attended the National Negro Convention in Buffalo and delivered his forceful address. After Garnet finished speaking to the 70 delegates in attendance, they held a lengthy and emotional debate on whether to endorse or reject his ideas. One of the delegates who disagreed with Garnet was the escaped slave and antislavery leader Frederick Douglass, who argued that Garnet's address, if circulated, would only lead to greater restrictions on free blacks in the South. In the end the resolution to accept the address was defeated by one vote.

For African Americans, slavery and racial discrimination continually raised deeply troubling philosophical and religious questions about the meaning of their experience, and in particular the injustice of their suffering. Black spokesmen, mainly ministers, struggled with this agonizing problem in sermons, speeches, and published addresses. In 1808, in one of the earliest surviving black sermons, Absalom Jones, rector of St. Thomas African Episcopal Church in Philadelphia, took up one of the most troubling questions: Why did God permit slavery? Perhaps it was God's plan, he suggested, that the descendants of the slaves learn Christianity "in order that they might become . . . messengers of it, to the land of their fathers."

It would be the divinely appointed task of African Americans to take the gospel of Christianity to Africa. And African Americans did become missionaries in Africa. David George, a black Baptist minister, fled Savannah, Georgia, in 1782 with the departing British forces and went to Nova Scotia. There he preached to other black immigrants and founded a Baptist church. In 1792, he migrated again, this time with a colony of African Americans to Sierra Leone on the west coast of Africa, where he formed another Baptist church. Daniel Coker, a leader of the African Methodist Episcopal Church in Baltimore and one of the founding members of the denomination in 1816, sailed to Sierra Leone in 1820 to preach the gospel and to engage in trade. Lott Carey and Colin Teague, two members of the African Baptist Missionary Society of Richmond, Virginia, were sent as missionaries to Liberia in 1821. African-American churches lacked the resources to sponsor large-scale missions to Africa, but the ideal of Christianizing Africa held great symbolic value for black Americans. The ideal provided them with a major role in the drama of world history and offered an explanation for African-American history: that God was drawing good out of the evil of slavery by using the American descendants of African slaves to take Christianity to the lands of their ancestors.

The discussion and definition of the historic role and destiny of black Americans became a major topic of sermons and speeches delivered by black clergy and community leaders during the first decades of the 19th century, especially on public ceremonial occasions, such as Freedom Day celebrations. Black communities held annual Freedom Day celebrations to commemorate three acts of emancipation that had already taken place: the abolition of the African slave trade to the United States on January 1, 1808, by an act of Congress; the abolition of slavery in New York State on July 4, 1827; and the emancipation of the British West Indies in 1834. These commemorations served as festive occasions for celebrating black solidarity and for interpreting the history and future destiny of African Americans. Not surprisingly, the black perspective on the meaning of American history differed drastically from that of whites.

At a time when white Americans took great pride in describing themselves as a "Redeemer Nation," chosen by God to spread Christianity and democracy around the world, black Americans were preaching that slavery made a mockery of the ideals of both Christianity and democracy. The United States, claimed Frederick Douglass and other antislavery orators, had created a false and hypocritical version of Christianity by compromising with the evil system of slavery.

The mission of black Christians was to convert the consciences of Americans to adopt the true Christian attitude of repentance for the sin of slavery. The fourth national Negro Convention in 1834 purposely compared the suffering of African Americans to the martyrdom of early Christians when it proclaimed that "our very sighs and groans like the blood of martyrs will prove to have been the seed of the church." And the American Moral Reform Society of 1837 spoke of black faces "as so many Bibles, that shall warn this guilty nation of her injustice." If the nation failed to listen, God would act as he had in Biblical times, warned Maria Stewart, a Boston antislavery activist, in 1831:

> America, foul and indelible is thy stain! Dark and dismal is the cloud that
> hangs over thee, for thy cruel wrongs and injuries to the fallen sons of Africa.
> The blood of her murdered ones cries to heaven for vengeance against Thee.

The End of the Slave Trade

Absalom Jones, leader of the Philadelphia black community, was ordained the first black Episcopal priest in 1804.

On January 1, 1808, Absalom Jones preached a Thanksgiving sermon to commemorate the abolition of the slave trade by the U.S. Congress on that day. He delivered the sermon at St. Thomas African Episcopal Church in Philadelphia, and it was later published. Jones makes a comparison between the enslavement of African Americans and the bondage of the children of Israel, an analogy that many black preachers have repeated right up to the present day.

The history of the world shows us that the deliverance of the children of Israel from their bondage is not the only instance in which it has pleased God to appear in behalf of oppressed and distressed nations, as the deliverer of the innocent, and of those who who call upon his name. . . . He has seen the affliction of our countrymen, with an eye of pity. . . . He has heard the prayers that have ascended from the hearts of his people; and he has, as in the case of his ancient and chosen people the Jews, *come down to deliver* our suffering countrymen from the hands of their oppressors. He *came down* into the United States, when they declared, in the constitution which they framed in 1788, that the trade in our African fellowmen should cease in the year 1808: He *came down* into the British Parliament, when they passed a law to put an end to the same iniquitous trade in May, 1807: He *came down* into the Congress of the United States, the last winter, when they passed a similar law, the operation of which commences on this happy day. Dear land of our ancestor! thou shalt no more be stained with the blood of thy children . . . the ocean shall no more afford a refuge to their bodies, from impending slavery: nor shall the shores of the British West India islands, and of the United States, any more witness the anguish of families, parted for ever by a publick sale. For this signal interposition of the God of mercies, in behalf or our brethren, it becomes us this day to offer up our united thanks.

AN

ORATION

ON

The Abolition of the Slave Trade;

DELIVERED

IN

THE AFRICAN CHURCH,

IN

THE CITY OF NEW-YORK,

JANUARY 1, 1808.

" Ethiopia shall soon stretch forth her hands unto God."
Psalm lxviii. 31.

" The people that walked in darkness have seen a great light.'
Isaiah ix. 2.

BY PETER WILLIAMS, JUN.
A DESCENDANT OF AFRICA.

New-York:

PRINTED BY SAMUEL WOOD.

NO. 362, PEARL-STREET.

1808.

Freedom-day celebrations honoring the 1808 abolition of the slave trade in the United States offered black preachers like Peter Williams, Jr., an occasion to speak about the history and the destiny of black people in the United States.

. . .You may kill, tyrannize, and oppress as much as you choose, until our cry shall come up before the throne of God; for I am firmly persuaded, that he will not suffer you to quell the proud, fearless and undaunted spirits of the Africans forever; for in his own time, he is able to plead our cause against you, and to pour out upon you the ten plagues of Egypt.

Stewart, who was born in Hartford, Connecticut, in 1803, moved to Boston in 1826, where she associated with David Walker and William Lloyd Garrison. She published several of her speeches in *The Liberator,* Garrison's abolitionist paper. An advocate of the rights of women, particularly African-American women, she participated in a black women's literary society, attended the Women's Anti-Slavery Convention of 1837, and lectured widely. Stewart taught school in New York City and Baltimore, and during the 1870s served as Matron (supervisor) of the Freedmen's Hospital in Washington, D.C., a position held earlier by Sojourner Truth. She died in 1879. In her active role as a lecturer and writer, she combined the issue of anti-slavery with the causes of black education and moral reform, insisting that African Americans devote themselves to educating and improving their communities "in the cause of God and the cause of freedom."

During the first three decades of the 19th century the independent black churches took on a variety of crucial roles. As sources of moral uplift, agencies of economic cooperation, arenas for political action, promoters of education, and houses of refuge in a hostile white world, the churches stood at the center of African-American community life.

Institutionally, the newly created churches grew in size and expanded with the spread of the nation. In 1817 the AME organization, with a membership of 6,784, had formed two regional districts, one in Philadelphia, the other in Baltimore, served by seven traveling ministers. By 1826 the organization had three regional districts and 17 traveling ministers, and its membership had reached 7,937. (The total would have included 3,000 more but for the destruction of the AME Church in Charleston, South Carolina, after the discovery of a slave plot to revolt.) By 1827 AME missionaries had begun to preach in Ohio, members from Bethel in Philadelphia had established an AME Church in Haiti, and four AME missions had been founded in Canada. In 1828, Morris Brown, former pastor of the Charleston church, was consecrated as the second bishop of the AME Church. In 1841, William Paul Quinn was appointed as assistant to Bishop Brown. Quinn, between 1840 and 1844, started 72 congregations, 47 churches, 40 temperance societies, 17 camp meetings, and 50 Sunday schools in Ohio, Indiana, Michigan, Illinois, Kentucky, and Missouri, the last two being slave states. In 1850, the Reverend Barney Fletcher organized St. Andrew's Church of Sacramento, the first AME congregation in California.

Jarena Lee wrote her autobiography to defend her right to preach the Christian gospel. She argued from the Bible and from the success of her own ministry that women could preach effectively.

Interdenominational disagreements and conflicts over issues of church politics accompanied the growth of the black churches. Rivalry between the African Methodist churches founded in Philadelphia and those organized in New York, for example, produced competition and led occasionally to territorial disputes. The growing congregations included large numbers of women, who made up an important part of the membership but were denied ordination and official license to preach, positions denied to women in white churches as well. One of the first black women to challenge the rule against women preaching was Jarena Lee, who wrote a narrative of her *Life and Religious Experience*, published in

1836. In it she argued that since Jesus had died to save the entire human race—women as well as men—there were no legitimate grounds for refusing women the right to preach his gospel. Lee served as a traveling revivalist, accepted by some male pastors and rejected by others.

In 1832, in Boston, Maria Stewart became one of the first American women, white or black, to deliver a public lecture on political issues to an audience made up of both men and women. She defended her right to do so by appealing to biblical precedents: "What if I am a woman; is not the God of ancient times the God of these modern days? Did he not raise up Deborah, to be a mother, and a judge in Israel? Did not Queen Esther save the lives of the Jews? And Mary Magdalene first declare the resurrection of Christ from the dead? . . . The religious spirit which has animated women in all ages . . . has made them by turns martyrs, apostles, warriors, and concluded in making them divines and scholars."

Another black woman who persisted in her religious ministry despite stiff opposition was Rebecca Cox Jackson, who emerged as a popular leader in weekly prayer meetings among black Methodists of Philadelphia in 1831. Motivated by visionary experiences, she began to attract large crowds of both sexes. As a result she was accused of improper conduct for leading men as well as women in prayer. In 1833 Jackson began a preaching tour to the towns and villages outside Philadelphia, and met with frequent resistance from congregations and ministers opposed to women preaching. After other disputes over doctrine, she broke with the AME Church. She joined the Shaker community in Watervliet, New York. The Shakers, officially called the United Society of Believers in Christ's Second Appearance, lived communally, practiced celibacy (abstained from sexual relations), and believed that Christ had returned in the person of their leader, "Mother" Ann Lee. Jackson returned to Philadelphia in 1851 to found a primarily black and mainly female Shaker community that she led until her death in 1871.

In 1848 the Daughters of Zion, an AME women's auxiliary society, petitioned the General Conference to grant official recognition to female preachers. Their petition was denied. A second petition in 1852 was also denied. The first black denomination to ordain a black woman was the African Methodist Episcopal Zion Church, which ordained Julia Foote in 1895.

Jarena Lee, Maria Stewart, Rebecca Cox Jackson, and other black women maintained considerable religious authority even though they could not serve as ordained pastors within the official structures of the black churches. Despite the opposition of church authorities, these women spoke out in public because they believed that they were directed by the Spirit of God. They defended their actions by pointing to the success their preaching ministry had in changing the lives of many people.

The independent church movement among African Americans gave black Christians the freedom to control their own churches, but many worshiped within churches led by white ministers or priests in denominations that had few, if any, black clergy. Sometimes this situation led to conflict, sometimes to mutual understanding and respect. African-American Christians firmly believed that Christianity ought to make no distinction on the basis of race or color, but they knew from bitter experience how often white American Christians fell short of that ideal. As long as black members were segregated in back pews and buried in separate sections of the graveyard, they were reminded how much the Christian churches had embraced the racism of the times instead of challenging it. When some of their strongest white allies in the antislavery movement failed to treat free blacks as fully equal people, they knew that the interracial community they longed for was still a distant goal.

Chapter 3

"The Invisible Institution": Religion Among the Slaves

During the antebellum period (1820–60), Christianity continued to grow among the slave population in the South. Some of this growth was institutional, as black churches continued to increase their membership, frequently recording the largest congregations in their local associations and far outnumbering many white congregations. But most Christian slaves had no access to black churches, and if they attended regular church services, they did so with white people. In fact it was common for slaves, seated in back pews or galleries, to outnumber white church members on any given Sunday in the antebellum South. But many slaves lived too far from churches to attend Sunday services regularly. If they were religiously inclined, some slaveholders hired a visiting clergyman to preach on their plantations, while others arranged set times to read to their slaves from printed sermons, prayer books, or Bible lessons.

The slaves, however, developed an extensive religious life that thrived outside the institutional church. Historians have called the slaves' religion an "invisible institution" because much of it was secret, invisible to the eyes of their masters. In their cabins, woods, thickets, hollows, and brush arbors (shelters of cut branches also called "hush harbors") throughout the South, slaves held their own religious meetings where they interpreted Christianity according to their experience, applying the stories and symbols of the Bible

Sunday was a day of relaxation and enjoyment for slaves, a holiday as well as a religious holy day. Music, dancing, and games—although condemned by the religious—served as a welcome relief from the toil of slavery.

One of the most important rituals of slave life, the funeral, was a solemn occasion in which the community mourned for the deceased and helped prepare him or her for the journey into the next world.

to make sense out of their lives. They were even willing to risk severe punishment to attend forbidden prayer meetings so they could worship God without white supervision and control. Out of the presence of whites, the slaves were free to express openly their desire for freedom in this life as well as the next.

The desire for "real preachin'," that is, sermons free of proslavery propaganda, pushed the slaves to hold their own religious gatherings. Former slave Lucretia Alexander described their disgust at the white preacher's version of the Gospel:

> The preacher came and . . . he'd just say, "Serve your masters. Don't steal your master's turkey. Don't steal your master's chickens. Don't steal your master's hawgs. Don't steal your master's meat. Do whatsomever your master tell you to do." Same old thing all the time. My father would have church in dwelling

houses and they had to whisper. . . . Sometimes they would have church at his house. That would be when they wanta real meetin' with some real preachin'. . . . They used to sing their songs in a whisper. That was a prayer meeting from house to house . . . once or twice a week.

As Henry Atkinson, an escaped slave from Virginia, put it, "The white clergymen don't preach the whole Gospel there."

Some slaveholders did permit their slaves to hold prayer meetings and enjoyed listening to the slaves' singing and preaching, but a basic contradiction distinguished the master's religion from that of the slaves. The difference can be most clearly seen in the black Christians' interpretation of the biblical story of Exodus. From the earliest period of their migration to America, British colonists had spoken of their journey across the Atlantic as the exodus of a New Israel from bondage in Egypt to the Promised Land of milk and honey. For African Americans the opposite was true: whites might claim that America was a new Israel, but blacks knew that it was Egypt because they, like the children of Israel of old, still toiled in bondage.

The special meaning that the story of Exodus held for the slaves was explained by a slave named Polly to her mistress: "We poor creatures have need to believe in God, for if God Almighty will not be good to us some day; why were we born? When I heard of his delivering his people from bondage I know it means the poor African." The story of Exodus contradicted the claim made by defenders of slavery that God intended Africans to be slaves. On the contrary, Exodus proved that slavery was against God's will and that slavery would end someday. The where and the how remained hidden in divine providence, but the promise of deliverance was certain. Moreover, the notion that blacks were inferior to whites was disproved by Exodus, which taught the slaves that they, like the Israelites of old, were a special people, chosen by God for deliverance.

The Christian slaves' identification with the biblical children of Israel was intensified by the songs, sermons, and prayers of their meetings, when the biblical past became dramatically present and the stories they sang about came alive. Once again God sent Moses to tell "ol' Pharaoh to let my people go." Once again the mighty wind of God parted the Red Sea so the Hebrew slaves could cross over dry land, while Pharaoh's army "got drownded." In the ecstasy of worship they reenacted the trials and triumphs of God's chosen people and so reaffirmed their own value and dignity, as they kept up their hope for freedom.

Drawing upon the worship traditions of Africa, as well as those of revivalistic Christianty, the slaves created services that resembled the spirit-empowered ceremonies of their African ancestors. Both traditions assumed that authentic worship required an observable experience of the divine presence. "It ain't enough to talk about God, you've got to feel him moving on the altar of your heart," as one former slave explained. Ritual, in this perspective, was supposed to bring the divine power tangibly into this world, so that people might be transformed, healed, and made whole. The presence of God became manifest in the words, the gestures, and the bodily movements of the believers. In this ecstatic form of African-American worship, the divine was embodied in the faithful. The emotional ecstasy of the slaves' worship services conveyed their belief that the whole person—body as well as spirit—made God present and so the human person became an image of God. By encouraging them to believe the biblical doctrine that everyone was created in the image of God, worship helped Christian slaves to fight off slavery's terrible power to depersonalize its victims.

An essential feature of the Protestant Christianity that most slaves accepted was the idea that one had to experience conversion to become a full member of the church. Events of great emotional and psychological power, conversions brought about a reorientation of the convert's life. "God struck me dead" was the vivid expression used by former slaves to describe the onset of conversion, an overwhelming feeling of inner transformation in which sadness, fear, and rejection changed to joy, confidence, and acceptance. Believing that God had chosen them to be saved, they spoke of conversion as an experience of rebirth, of being made entirely new, of being filled with love for everything and everybody. They felt that they were of infinite worth as children of God, no matter what slaveholders thought and taught. For those facing the brutal conditions of slavery—the daily physical, psychological, and emotional attacks against

their worth as a person—to experience the acceptance and affirmation of God renewed their sense of value and importance.

Slave preachers led the meetings of the "invisible institution" and exercised a good deal of influence among the slaves in general. Although most were illiterate, their verbal artistry earned the slave preachers the respect of blacks and sometimes whites as well. The slave preacher had to be careful not to mention freedom or equality for black people in this life, but only in Heaven—at least in the presence of whites. Preachers and their followers developed ingeniously indirect and veiled references to fool any whites who might be listening. A song like "Steal Away," for example, with its words "Steal Away, Steal Away to Jesus/Steal Away, Steal Away Home," might be used to announce a secret prayer meeting without the overseer catching on.

Many slave preachers practiced a style of revivalistic preaching that has come to be called the "chanted" sermon because of its rhythmic

The expression of emotion in black religious services moved some observers to tears, while others laughed or made fun of black worship. For many black Christians, true worship required that you "feel [the power of God] moving on the altar of your heart," as one slave put it.

structure and musical tone. In this kind of sermon, the preacher began calmly and slowly and then gradually built to a quicker, more excited pace, his words set to a regular beat reinforced by the congregation's shouts of "Amen" or "Preach it." Finally, he reached an emotional peak in which the chanted words of the sermon merged with the singing, clapping, and shouting of the congregation. The effect of this style of sermon was to heighten the emotional power of the preacher's message as he and his congregation spurred each others' religious fervor by their mutual interaction.

As in regular churches, slave women were not preachers in the "invisible institution," but they exercised religious authority nonetheless. Some served their communities as experts in the healing arts, combining the use of herbal medicine with prayer and religious ritual to assist the sick, the dying, and women experiencing childbirth. Others acted as "spiritual mothers," respected for their spiritual wisdom and gifts of insight, including the ability to explain people's dreams and to advise them on the state of their souls. Women assigned to care for young slave children (and sometimes white children also) gave them their first instruction in Christian prayers, songs, and stories.

Hindered from learning to read and write by law or by custom, slaves learned the Bible by hearing it preached. Bible passages were memorized and became part of the slaves' folktales. In particular, the songs known as spirituals brought the biblical characters and stories vividly to life. Spirituals brought together Protestant hymns and African music styles into a distinctly creative and expressive synthesis. People sang them at work and at prayer, in groups and alone. Spirituals were not only sung, but they engaged the whole body in hand-clapping, foot-stamping, head-shaking excitement. And they were danced in the counterclockwise, circular shuffle known as the "ring shout." As they circled around in a ring, the slaves moved into states of religious trance that left them renewed in spirit.

The words of the spirituals could hold different meanings for different people. A verse might speak of freedom from sin and, at the same time, also refer to freedom from slavery. They were used to give signals and to offer warnings. As Frederick Douglass noted, the line "O Canaan, sweet Canaan, I am bound for the land of Canaan" meant "something more than a hope of reaching heaven," to him and several slave companions as they made plans to escape from slavery. "We meant to reach the *North*, and the North was our Canaan." Frequently slaves created these songs spontaneously, with one singer making up verses and the group adding a chorus familiar to all. The flexible structure of the spirituals allowed the slaves to comment on the daily events of their lives, so that the community heard and shared the cares and burdens of the individual expressed through song.

The spirituals reflected upon life's sorrows and its joys:

> One morning I was walking down
> I saw some berries hanging down,
> I pick de berry and I suck de juice,
> Just as sweet as the honey in de comb.
> Sometimes I'm up, sometimes I'm down
> Sometimes I'm almost on de groun'.

The slaves sang of the power of God to deliver them just as he had delivered his people of old:

> O my Lord delivered Daniel
> O why not deliver me too?

In songs of haunting beauty, anonymous slave communities captured the poignancy of the human condition, which affected the master no less than the slave:

> I know moon-rise, I know star-rise
> Lay dis body down.
> I walk in de moonlight,
> I walk in de starlight,
> To lay dis body down.
> I'll walk through de graveyard,
> To lay dis body down.
> I'll lie in de grave and
> stretch out my arms;
> Lay dis body down.
> I go to de judgment in de
> evenin' of de day,

Muslim slaves in South Carolina and Georgia remembered the Islamic traditions they had practiced in Africa. Imprisoned as a runaway, Omar ibn Said gained great fame by writing on his cell walls in Arabic.

When I lay dis body down;
And my soul and your soul
will meet in de day
When I lay dis body down.

The wisdom and humanity of these slave songs have touched people around the world.

The spirituals, the experience of conversion, and the chanted sermon characterized the Protestant worship practiced by the majority of Christian slaves; but not all slaves were Protestant—or, for that matter, Christian. There were Muslim slaves in the South who continued to observe the prayers and devotions of Islam as best they could. According to their descendants, Bilali Mahomet and his wife, Phoebe, slaves on Sapelo Island, Georgia, prayed very regularly at dawn, noon, and sunset; they faced east (toward Mecca) and used a prayer mat and prayer beads. Omar (or Umar) ibn Said, a slave in North Carolina, wrote an autobiographical statement in Arabic script in 1831 that recalled his Muslim past in Africa:

> Before I came to the Christian country, my religion was the religion of Mohammed, the Apostle of God—may God have mercy upon him and give him peace! I walked to the mosque before day-break, washed my face and head and hands and feet. I prayed at noon, prayed in the afternoon, prayed at sunset, prayed in the evening. I gave alms every year . . . I went on pilgrimage to Mecca . . . When I left my country I was thirty-seven years old; I have been in the country of the Christians twenty-four years.

Muslim slaves, few in number, were isolated in a society that was overwhelmingly Christian and ignorant of Islam.

There were relatively few Roman Catholic slaves as well, except in southern Louisiana and Maryland, the two areas of North America where significant slave and white Catholic populations came into contact. John Carroll, the first American bishop, reported in 1785 that about 3,000 of the 15,800 Catholics in Maryland were slaves. Small populations of black

Catholics emerged in areas of Kentucky settled by Catholic slaveholders from Maryland. In New Orleans and Baltimore, French-speaking free "people of color"—as they called themselves—formed important communities of black Catholics, enlarged after 1792 by refugees from the revolution in Haiti. In these two cities, two communities of black nuns were organized, the Oblate Sisters of Providence in 1829 in Baltimore and the Sisters of the Holy Family in 1842 in New Orleans. They educated black children, cared for the elderly and the sick, and served an important symbolic role for black Catholics, since black priests were so rare.

The first black Americans ordained to the priesthood were James, Patrick, and Alexander Sherwood Healy, the sons of a slave mother and her Irish immigrant master. Born in Georgia, all three were sent North to be educated, first at a Quaker school on Long Island, New York, and then at Holy Cross College in Massachusetts. All three did their seminary training abroad and were ordained in Europe. James became bishop of Portland, Maine; Patrick, a Jesuit, served as president of Georgetown University in Washington, D.C.; Alexander Sherwood taught in the provincial (regional) seminary in Troy, New York. The racial background of the Healys was generally known, but they were not publicly acclaimed as black priests and did not work among black Catholics. Though a black Protestant clergy emerged in the late 19th century, it took another century for a black Catholic priest to be ordained in the United States.

The strongest alternative to Protestantism among the slaves was the tradition of conjure. A combination of religion, medicine, magic, and folklore, conjure flourished in the slave quarters. The appeal of conjure depended upon its effectiveness in explaining illness and misfortune and its prescriptions for curing them. Slaves, and surprising numbers of white people, believed that the conjurer had the power to cure but also to harm. Conjurers, also called root doctors or hoodoo (a word derived from "voodoo") doctors, used materials (such as roots, herbs, bones, and graveyard dirt) whose spiritual power was activated by secret spells known only to the conjurer. A variety of otherwise unexplained illnesses, mental and physical, or a series of accidents were blamed upon conjure.

The three Healy brothers (James, Alexander, and Patrick) were all ordained as Catholic priests in the 19th century and served communities in Portland (Maine), Boston, and Washington, D.C.

An African-style drum found in Virginia before 1753 represents the ongoing significance of African culture, even when prohibited, upon slaves and their descendants in America.

Conjurers possessed an air of mystery and of power based upon the widespread belief that any spell placed by a conjurer could be removed only by a conjurer; a medical doctor was useless. If called in time, the root doctor took several steps to effect a cure. Once he had determined that the patient had indeed been conjured, he needed to discover where the charm had been hidden and to identify the person who had ordered the conjuring done. Curing the patient depended upon destroying or counteracting the power of the charm. Since most conjurers had expert knowledge of herbs, medicinal potions and ointments made up part of the cure. The final step, if the patient so wished, was to seek revenge by turning the charm against the person who sent it.

Christian slaves sometimes spoke of conjure as evil, the tool of the devil. But many conjurers were themselves religious and regarded their skill as a gift from God. Some slaves were skeptical about the conjurer's claims to power. But, whatever their views, slaves troubled by illness or misfortune might put aside their objections to conjure in their search for a remedy for their suffering.

African religious traditions continued within and alongside Christian practices among the slaves. The effects of these traditions can be seen most clearly in slave worship, burial, and conjure. The ring shout, the circular counterclockwise movement that inspired religious trances among the slaves, closely resembled religious dances in Africa, the Caribbean, and Brazil that also brought worshipers into states of trance. While slaves were forbidden to use drums because of slave codes in the United States, their clapping and chanting duplicated the rhythmic drive of the drums that was so crucial in African worship. Similarly, the singing style of the slaves was strongly influenced by patterns of African song: call and response, multiple rhythms, syncopation (stressing the off or weak beat of a rhythm), slides from one note to another, repetition, hand-clapping, and body movement.

From the people of the Kongo, who constituted perhaps one-third to one-half of the Africans imported into the United States, slaves transmitted the custom of placing the personal belongings of the deceased upon the grave, bordering the grave with white shells or other objects, and planting a tree directly on the grave. In African-American graveyards, cups, saucers, pipes, and other possessions of the deceased, often those last used before death, were placed on the grave for the person's spirit. Setting a border around the grave marked it off as a place of spiritual power, a passageway between the world of the living and the world of the spirits. White shells represented the sea, the border between the two worlds. Trees represented the ongoing cycle of life, death, and rebirth.

The belief that human illness and misfortune could be caused by the ill will of others acting through charms assembled by conjurers was widespread in both Africa and Europe. Slaves emphasized the African roots of conjure and viewed Africa as a place particularly strong in magic, and conjurers frequently bragged of their African origin to guarantee their expertise and authenticity. Certain ways of wrapping charms with red cloth and specific ingredients, such as "goopher" (graveyard) dust, originated in Africa. Nevertheless, conjure was one area in which European and African traditions resembled and thus reinforced one another.

In fact, in the United States African religions and Christianity came to be more closely and inseparably interwoven than in any other slave society in the Americas. Religions like Vodou in Haiti and Santería in Cuba adopted Catholic imagery but remained fundamentally African in character. To their followers in those countries Catholicism constituted a parallel religious system, which they might also practice on certain occasions, but in a separate place and at a separate time. The parish church remained distinct from the Vodou or Santería house of worship. In the United States, on the other hand, Christian conversion and the ring-shout occurred in the same prayer meetings as the slaves joined Protestant revivalism and African ritual dance into a single religious ceremony. Why the difference?

The Catholics of the French colony of St. Domingue (Haiti) and the Spanish colony of Cuba focused a great deal of their religious devotion on the Virgin Mary and the saints. The slaves defined the Catholic saints as European equivalents of African spirits and adapted their images to represent (and, if necessary, to mask) their service to the gods of Africa. Because the Protestants of British North America rejected the veneration of saints as a form of idolatry, the slaves lacked a source of images to cloak and to represent the personalities of African gods and spirits.

However, unlike the Catholic Mass, the Protestant revival meeting did present the slaves with an equivalent to the ceremonial dances and ritual spirit trances of Africa. In Protestant prayer meetings, slaves moved, sang, and worshiped in ways remarkably similar to those of Africa.

Moreover, the pattern of slave distribution influenced the religions of slaves in the United States and in the Caribbean islands to develop in different directions. The distribution of Africans imported into the Western Hemisphere was not uniform. Of the total number, it is estimated that only around 4.5 percent were brought to North America. The island of Haiti imported more than twice as many slaves as the United States, and Cuba received more slaves in the first half of the 19th century than the United States did overall. Also, slaves in these Caribbean islands were concentrated in small geographic areas, as opposed to the wide dispersal of slaves in the United States. The slave populations working the plantations of Haiti and Cuba were much larger than the white populations of French or Spanish settlers. In the United States, large concentrations of slaves were comparatively rare and the slaves lived amidst a white population that was equal or larger in size, with the exception of Louisiana and the coastal areas of Georgia and South Carolina.

In addition, the slave population in the United States had a much higher rate of natural increase compared to slave populations in the rest of the Americas. The mortality rate of slaves in the Caribbean exceeded their overall birthrate, so in order to maintain the slave population, Caribbean slaveholders had to import slaves from Africa continually. This ongoing importation meant that the Caribbean slave population was continuously re-Africanized. On the other hand, most Africans brought to the United States arrived between 1750 and 1808, the year the

slave trade officially ended. Although slaves continued to be secretly imported by smugglers after 1808, their numbers were nowhere near the size of the African population imported into Cuba, for example, until the 1860s. And unlike in the Caribbean, the birthrate of slaves in the United States exceeded their death rate. As a result, by the 19th century the bulk of the slave population in North America was native-born, and a relatively small number of Africans found themselves enslaved in the midst of a rapidly increasing native-born population whose memories of the African past grew fainter with each passing generation. The influx of African cultural influence, therefore, was far less extensive in the United States than in the Caribbean.

"The Preacher is the most unique personality developed by the Negro on American soil. A leader, a politician, an orator, a 'boss,' an intriguer, an idealist—all these he is, and ever, too, the centre of a group of men, now twenty, now a thousand in number," wrote W.E.B. DuBois in *The Souls of Black Folk* (1903).

These differences in slave population and cultural influence had a major impact upon the religious lives of the slaves. In the Caribbean, the continuous importation of large numbers of African slaves during the 19th century supported the development of African-based religions outside the Catholic Church. In the United States, the rapid growth of an American-born slave population and the close of the African slave trade in 1808 supported the development of an Africanized revivalistic Protestantism.

Slaveholders had mixed feelings about the religion of their slaves. They continued to wonder about the effects of Christianity upon their slaves' attitude toward slavery: Did Christianity make slaves accept their condition, or did it make them resist slavery? Most slaves had to keep publicly silent about their attitudes, but in private they condemned the injustice of slavery and expected that justice would be done to slaveholders in the world to come. As Frederick Douglass noted, "Slaves knew enough of the orthodox theology of the time to consign all bad slaveholders to hell." In the hereafter, the slaves predicted, there would be a reversal of the conditions of whites and blacks.

The slaves condemned the religion of the masters as hypocritical and refused to obey moral rules held up to them by whites, especially commands against stealing. While white preachers repeatedly urged "Don't steal," slaves denied that this commandment applied to them, since they themselves were stolen property. Former slave Josephine Howard explained how the moral system preached by whites collapsed when examined from the slaves' point of view: "Dey allus done tell us it am wrong to lie and steal, but why did de white foks steal my mammy and her mammy? Dey lives clost to some water, somewheres over in Africy, and de man come in a little boat to de sho' and tell dem he got presents in de big boat . . . and my mammy and her mammy gits took out to dat big boat and day locks dem in a black hole what mammy say so black you can't see nothin'. Dat de sinfulles' stealin' dey is." Slaves reasoned that to take from their masters was not stealing because they had a right to the produce of their own labor. The slaves' own moral code, however, carefully distinguished between "taking" from the master and "stealing" from another slave, which was regarded as the worst kind of sin. Lying and deception, wrong under normal circumstances, became under slavery necessary tools for survival. "Puttin' on ol' massa," by hiding one's real feelings and by masking the truth when dealing with whites became an important part of the slaves' code of protecting themselves and one another.

Religious duty and a sense of moral superiority occasionally led some slaves to act in the master's interest rather than their own. But religious faith also sustained the decisions of slaves to flee or to revolt, convinced that God would protect and assist them. In 1822, a former slave named Denmark Vesey organized a plot to revolt among slaves in the vicinity of Charleston, South Carolina. Vesey reportedly appealed to the Bible to convert recruits to join his cause, and most of the leaders of the planned rebellion were active members of Charleston's African Methodist Church, which was disbanded and destroyed by the white city officials after the plot was discovered. The pastor of the church, Morris Brown, was suspected of involvement in the plot and had to flee North to escape prosecution. One of the leaders, a conjurer from Africa named Gullah Jack, gave his men a charm that was supposed to make them invulnerable to the white people's guns. Thus the Vesey conspiracy had the backing of both Christianity and conjure. Nat Turner, the leader of the bloodiest slave revolt in the history of the nation, was viewed by his fellow slaves as a preacher, healer, and seer. Turner claimed that God had used certain signs in the heavens to instructed him to strike in 1831 against the whites of Northampton, Virginia.

Christianity, as slaveholders had all along suspected, was a double-edged sword. Even though the Bible did not condemn slavery explicitly, the book of Exodus and the passages from the prophets that depicted the struggle of Israel against stronger nations supplied the slaves with images of resistance, as well as ammunition for outright rebellion. Practicing religion itself could be for slaves an act of resistance—an assertion of independence that sometimes required defiance of the master's commands. When the master's will conflicted with God's, over attending a prayer meeting, for example, slaves faced a choice: obey God or obey man. Strengthened by the belief that salvation lay in obeying God rather than man, some slaves chose to disobey their masters. Beatings did not stop slaves from praying, and these prayers were symbols of resistance.

However, some slaves resisted slavery by rejecting Christianity itself as a white man's religion. They could not accept belief in a supposedly just God who could will or permit slavery. A freedwoman named Nellie admitted in an interview in 1864, "it has been a terrrible mystery, to know why the good Lord should so long afflict my people, and keep them in bondage,—to be abused, and trampled down, without any rights of their own,—with no ray of light in the future." Though she had refused to despair, she reported of others: "Some of my folks said there wasn't any God, for if there was he wouldn't let white folks do as they have done for so many years."

Two extremes of behavior, accommodation and rebelliousness, have dominated the discussion about slave personality and the slave-master relationship. But these were not the only alternatives. The Christianity that many slaves and masters practiced occasionally led to moments of genuine religious interdependence, whereby blacks and whites preached to, prayed for, and converted each other in situations where the status of master and slave was, at least for the moment, forgotten. In the fervor of religious worship, master and slave, white and black, sometimes shared a common sermon, professed a common faith, and experienced a common ecstasy.

Slave religion has been stereotyped as otherworldly, distracting slaves from doing something about their situation in this life. It was otherworldly in the sense that it taught that this world and this life were not the end, nor were they the final measure of existence. To decide that religion distracted slaves from concern with this life and persuaded them not to act in the present fails to acknowledge the full story. Slave religion had a this-worldly impact because it helped slaves to experience their own personal value. The religious meetings in the quarters, groves, and "hush harbors" were themselves frequently acts of resistance against the orders of the masters. By obeying the commands of God instead of the commands of men, slaves acted according to their own consciences independent of their masters. In the role of preacher, slaves achieved respect, authority, and power. The conversion experience equipped the slave with a sense of importance that counteracted the dehumanizing force of slavery. In their prayer meetings, slaves enjoyed community and fellowship, which transformed their individual sorrows into moments of joy. In the midst of slavery, they treasured these and other ways in which religion brought meaning, hope, and inner freedom to their lives.

Chapter 4

In Search of Canaan: Emancipation and the Limits of Freedom

Both the North and the South regarded the Civil War as a holy war, a sacred cause. The sectional controversy over slavery had already split two of the nation's largest religious denominations. The Methodist Church divided into Northern and Southern branches over the issue of slavery in 1844 with the creation of the Methodist Episcopal Church, South. Northern and Southern Baptists broke in 1845, resulting in the formation of the Southern Baptist Convention. The religious aspects of the conflict were heightened by prayer meetings and revivals that occured among Union and Confederate troops. "Battle Hymn of the Republic," composed by Julia Ward Howe in 1862, expressed the religious idealism of the Union cause:

> Mine eyes have seen the glory of
> the coming of the Lord.
> He is trampling out the vintage
> where the grapes of wrath are stored.
> He has loosed the fearful lightning of
> his terrible swift sword.
> His truth goes marching on.
> Glory, Glory, Hallelujah!
> Glory, Glory, Hallelujah!
> Glory, Glory, Hallelujah!
> His truth goes marching on.

After emancipation African Americans continued to practice the rituals of the religious culture of their parents and grandparents. Group baptisms in rivers are part of the long history of slave religion.

Henry McNeal Turner, an AME minister (and later bishop), was one of the first black chaplains in the Civil War. After the war he briefly held political office in Georgia before returning to full-time pastoral work in the church.

Northern blacks demanded that they be allowed to fight in the war, and when regiments of African-American soldiers were finally organized, black pastors such as AME minister Henry McNeal Turner eagerly signed up as chaplains.

In the South, slaves learned that the long-awaited moment had come—the fight for their freedom had begun. As the war progressed they had to hide their true feelings, especially their frequent prayers for the success of the North's armies. But when the end of the war appeared certain, they let the mask drop and, as Booker T. Washington, the founder of Tuskegee Institute and the most prominent national black leader of his generation, later recalled:

> As the great day grew nearer, there was more singing in the slave quarters than usual. It was bolder, had more ring, and lasted later into the night. Most of the verses of the plantation songs had some reference to freedom. True, they had sung those same verses before, but they had been careful to explain that the "freedom" in these songs referred to the next world, and had no connection with life in this world. Now they gradually threw off the mask; and were not afraid to let it be known that the "freedom" in their songs meant freedom of the body in this world.

Emancipation, at long last, seemed to fulfill the hopes and prayers of generations, as the newly freed slaves sang the hymn:

> Shout the glad tidings o'er Egypt's dark sea
> Jehovah has triumphed, his people are free!

The former slaves' joy was shadowed by uncertainty, by delay, by dislocation, disruption, chaos, and poverty. What did freedom in fact mean? The desperate situation of thousands of newly freed slaves could only be met by organized efforts for relief.

Groups of concerned whites and blacks set up freedman's aid societies to provide material assistance. In addition to the Freedman's Bureau of the Federal Government, several denominations set up freedman's aid agencies to raise money and to send agents and teachers into the South. One of the most active and effective of these agencies was the American Missionary Association (AMA), founded under the auspices of the Congregational Church. By 1868, the AMA had 532 missionaries and teachers working among the former slaves in the South with a budget of about $400,000 a year. The AMA journal, the *American Missionary,* regularly reported to a wide audience on the situation of the freedmen.

Black churches also joined the effort to assist the former slaves. In cities with large black populations, church-based freedman's aid societies sprang up, such as the Union Relief Association founded by the Israel Bethel Church of Washington, D.C., led by Henry McNeal Turner. Bethel Church in Philadelphia established the Contraband Committee to aid blacks who had escaped slavery by seeking refuge behind the Union Army's lines (these people were called "contrabands," or seized property of war). In New York City, the African Civilization Society, founded in 1858 by Henry Highland Garnet and others to promote missions to Africa, took on the activities of a freedman's aid society during and after the war.

Henry McNeal Turner recorded the names of black troops assigned to him as chaplain in the Union Army in this roll book.

Besides tangible relief from want, another major need of the newly freed slaves was education. The former slaves demonstrated an intense desire to learn to read and to "figure" (do arithmetic) because they fervently believed that there was a direct connection between education and freedom. For people who had been prohibited from learning to read and write as slaves, reading offered tangible proof that they were really free.

Harriet Ware, a white Northern teacher in Port Royal, Virginia, noticed the religious awe with which the freed people viewed education. Attending a funeral in 1862, she observed: "As we drew near to the grave we heard all the children singing their A,B,C, through and through again, as they stood waiting round the grave . . . Each child had his school-book or picture book . . . in his hand,—another proof that they consider their lessons as in some sort religious exercises." The desire to read the Bible for themselves—the Bible the slaveholders had so long misrepresented to them—motivated a good many former slaves to seek education.

For Northern teachers, whether white or black, education had a

White missionaries and schoolteachers came South after the war to educate the former slaves. Laura M. Towne posed with some of her newly freed pupils on St. Helena Island, South Carolina, in 1866.

moral purpose. In addition to reading, writing, and arithmetic, they believed schools ought to instill habits of thrift, honesty, punctuality, temperance, and discipline in the ex-slaves, who seemed to be lax about these moral virtues. The former slaves, however, insisted that God was not going to punish them for every little sin. For them the essence of religion was not in observing rules and regulations, but in experiencing the power of God's grace within their hearts.

As well-intentioned Northerners tried to teach New England values to rural blacks, wide differences in education and background began to appear. Problems of misunderstanding occurred as Northerners struggled to understand Southern black speech, customs, and attitudes that differed from their own. Out of the educational efforts of these missionary-teachers and the efforts of the former slaves themselves a number of black freedman's schools developed despite the obstacles of misunderstanding, poverty, and occasional opposition from Southern whites.

From small, unimpressive beginnings, several of the freedman's schools grew over the years into major black educational institutions of long-lasting importance. Some of the historically black colleges and universities that originated in modest freedman's aid schools funded by white churches are Shaw University, Raleigh, North Carolina, opened in 1865 (Baptist); Morehouse College, Atlanta, Georgia, in 1867 (Baptist); Morgan, now Morgan State, Baltimore, Maryland, in 1867 (Methodist); Fisk University, Nashville, Tennessee, in 1866 (AMA); Talladega, Talladega, Alabama, in 1867 (AMA); Hampton Institute, Hampton, Virginia, in 1868 (AMA); and Knoxville College, Knoxville, Tennessee, in 1875 (Presbyterian). Schools founded by black churches included Morris Brown, Atlanta, in 1885 (AME); and Livingstone College, Salisbury,

North Carolina, in 1879 (AME Zion). Many black-funded schools promoted a philosophy of industrial education, a practical or vocational program designed to instill the primary virtue of industriousness as the key to moral development. Their goal was to teach students how to earn a living and how to live a morally respectable life. This ideal of industrial education for black people had widespread influence due to its chief spokesman, Booker T. Washington, himself a former slave. Washington, educated at Hampton Institute in Virginia, founded the Tuskegee Institute in Alabama and built it into an institution of national reputation, influence, and power that still exists today.

Industrial education strove to instill character—that is, Yankee virtues of industry, thrift, and self-reliance—in the Southern black population. It sought to adjust the freed people to the civic life of the United States by indoctrinating them in the traditional values of middle-class Protestantism, a task embraced wholeheartedly by black and white Northern missionaries. The white and black clergy who came South to minister to the former slaves were shocked by what they perceived to be the freedmen's "primitive, barbaric, and heathenish" religion, as AME bishop Daniel Alexander Payne put it. They were upset by the ring shout and by the excessive emotionalism of the former slaves' worship. They were also critical of the "immoral piety" of the former slaves, who explicitly objected to sermons urging them to obey the Ten Commandments. The Northern missionaries failed to understand that the freed people's disdain for preaching about morality was a reaction to the white preaching they had endured during slavery. The former slaves preferred to focus on feeling the power of God's love, in the tradition of the invisible institution of their parents and grandparents.

The arrival of Northern missionaries in the South occasionally created resentment and conflict. White missionaries sponsored by the Northern Congregationalists, Methodists, Presbyterians, and Baptists alienated Southern whites, who criticized them as Yankee interlopers. And black missionaries resented competition from their white rivals in adding freed people to their churches' rolls. Black missionaries saw this field as their particular mission even before the Civil War ended.

The African Methodist Episcopal Church, the first to enter the South, was particularly effective in organizing congregations. Less than 48 hours after General William Tecumseh Sherman had taken Savannah, Georgia, on December 21, 1864, James Lynch entered the city and persuaded the black congregation of Andrews Chapel, affiliated with the Southern Methodists, to join the AME Church. Lynch reported of his experience working with the freed people of South Carolina: "Ignorant though they be, on account of long years of oppression, they exhibit a desire to hear and to learn that I never imagined. Every word you say while preaching, they drink down and respond to, with an earnestness that sets your heart all on fire, and you feel that it is indeed God's work to minister to them."

Lynch was followed into the South by other AME ministers and by Bishop Daniel Alexander Payne, who returned from Wilberforce, Ohio, to his native Charleston in 1865 to organize the South Carolina Conference of the AME Church. Payne's return was deeply satisfying because he had been forced to leave the city 30 years earlier when his school for free black children was declared illegal by the state legislature. AME growth was so rapid that by 1878 it was necessary to divide South Carolina into two conferences. In 1865, the cornerstone was laid for a new AME Church in Charleston, replacing the structure that had been destroyed in the aftermath of Denmark Vesey's conspiracy in 1822. The architect of the new church was Robert Vesey, Denmark's son.

By 1866, there were 11 black churches in Charleston: five Methodist, two Presbyterian, two Episcopalian, one Congregational, and one Baptist. Class, status, and color distinctions that were of long standing within the black community of Charleston were reflected in the membership of these different churches. Lighter-skinned blacks, the children of interracial relationships between white and black parents, were more likely to have been free than darker-skinned blacks, due to the decision of a white parent or relative to emancipate them. Lighter-skinned free blacks also tended to be wealthier than darker-skinned ones, and they enjoyed more opportunities for education. Southern white society viewed the physical features of white people as attractive and the skin color, hair texture, and facial features of black people as ugly. In this racist view, lighter skin and

"Go ye into all the world and preach the Gospel to every creature." Mark xvi, 15.

"Exhort with all long-suffering and doctrine."

This is to Certify, That the bearer *Benjamin J. Jam* 18

is licensed to **Preach** *in the* AFRICAN METHODIST EPISCOPAL CHURCH:

Signed in behalf of the **Quarterly** Conference of said Church, so long as his life corresponds with the Gospel and he submit to the rules of the Discipline of said Church.—To be renewed once a year,

Given under my hand, this *13* day of *December* in the year of our Lord one thousand eight hundred and *58*

John Tibbs Pastor Wylie St. Charge, P. Mabury

Euro-American features made a black person seem more intelligent and more respectable. In Charleston, some of the lighter-skinned free "people of color" set themselves apart from other blacks as a distinct group with their own social organizations, associations, and churches.

As a result of their missions, Northern black denominations in effect became national churches as they increased in size and geographical extent. For example, between 1860 and 1870 the AME Zion Church increased in membership from 27,000 to 200,000, with the great bulk of its growth in the South. By 1880 the AME Church had grown to 400,000 members, most of them Southern blacks. But by far the largest institutional growth was achieved by the black Baptists, and it did not require missionaries from the North.

Following the Union Army's victory, black Baptists swarmed out of Southern Baptist Churches. To take one example, in 1858 the Southern Baptist Conference in South Carolina counted 29,211 black members; in 1874 there were 1,614. Black Baptists simply withdrew and formed their own congregations. Gradually they formed state associations (North Carolina in 1866, followed by Alabama and Virginia in 1867). Eventually, a National Baptist Convention was formed in 1895. Meanwhile, former slaves who had belonged to the Southern Methodist Church withdrew into AME or AME Zion churches, or they joined a new black Methodist

This license to preach was issued by the AME Church in 1858. After the Civil War, the AME Church spread to the South, gaining members and growing in size.

Christianity vs. Slavery

Daniel Alexander Payne was born to free parents in Charleston, South Carolina, in 1811. Educated at a school established by free blacks, he studied mathematics, French, Latin, and Greek. In 1829 he opened his own school for black children and taught there until 1834, when the state legislature passed a law against teaching slaves or free blacks to read or write. With his school closed, Payne traveled north to study at the Lutheran Theological Seminary in Gettysburg, Pennsylvania, and became a Lutheran minister in 1839. At his ordination, Payne delivered this antislavery speech, which described the conflict between slavery and Christianity.

Payne left the Lutherans in 1841 to join the African Methodist Episcopal Church, where he was elected bishop in 1852. As bishop he spoke out for greater education among ministers and led in the founding of a black college, Wilberforce University in Ohio, in 1856. From 1863 to 1879 he served as president of Wilberforce. He died in 1893.

The slaves are sensible of the oppression exercised by their masters; and they see these masters on the Lord's day worshiping in His holy Sanctuary. They hear their masters professing Christianity; they see their masters preaching the Gospel; they hear these masters praying in their families, and they know that oppression and slavery are inconsistent with the Christian religion; therefore they scoff at religion itself—mock their masters, and distrust both the goodness and justice of God. Yes, I have known them even to question His existence. I speak not of what others have told me, but of what I have both seen and heard from the slaves themselves. I have heard the mistress ring the bell for family prayer, and I have seen the servants immediately begin to sneer and laugh; and have heard them declare they would not go in to prayers, adding, if I go in she will only just read, "Servants obey your masters"; but she will not read, "Break every yoke, and let the oppressed go free." I have seen colored men at the church door, scoffing at the ministers, while they were preaching, and saying, you had better go home, and set your slaves free. A few nights ago between ten and eleven o'clock a runaway slave came to the house where I live for safety and succor. I asked him if he was a Christian. "No sir," said he, "white men treat us so bad in Mississippi that we can't be Christians." . . . I taught school in Charleston five years. In 1834 the legislature of our state enacted a law to prohibit colored teachers. My school was filled with children and youth of the most promising talents; and when I looked upon them and remembered that in a few more weeks this school shall be closed and I be permitted no more to teach them . . . I began to question the existence of the Almighty and to say, if indeed there is a God, does he deal justly? Is he a just God? Is he a holy Being? If so, why does he permit a handful of dying men thus to oppress us? Why does he permit them to hinder me from teaching these children, when nature, reason and Revelation commanded me to teach them?

AME bishop Daniel Alexander Payne, one of the foremost advocates of education for blacks in the 19th century, became president of Wilberforce, a black university in Ohio, and then returned to his native Charleston after the Civil War to organize the AME church there.

Reverend Hiram R. Revels served as a missionary in the South after the war and was elected to the Mississippi State Senate in 1869. In 1870 he became the first African American elected to the U.S. Senate.

denomination, the Colored (later renamed Christian) Methodist Episcopal Church, which separated from the Methodist Episcopal Church in 1870. In South Carolina, the black membership of the Southern Methodists fell from 42,469 in 1860 to 653 in 1873.

Ministers took an active role in politics during the period of Reconstruction as a matter of course because they were the major profession within the black community and they were trained in the oratorical and organizational skills needed for political leadership. Jesse Freeman Boulden, for example, served as pastor of Zion Baptist Church in Chicago until the war turned in the North's favor. He organized a missionary association in Illinois to plan ways of following the Union Army into the South, where he hoped to found churches among the freedmen. In 1865, he resigned his pastorate and moved to Natchez, Mississippi, where he immediately got involved in the political organization of the state. He presented a petition to Congress that requested the vote for black men in Mississippi. He was elected to the state legislature in Mississippi and helped guide the election of Hiram Revels to the U.S. Senate in 1870. (Revels filled the seat vacated by Confederate president Jefferson Davis.) Meanwhile Boulden continued to serve various churches and edited a religious newspaper, *The Baptist Reflector.*

AME minister Richard Harvey Cain traveled to South Carolina after the war. In Charleston, he organized Emmanuel AME Church, which grew to 4,000 members. He edited a Republican newspaper, became a member of the Reconstruction constitutional convention in South Carolina, served for two years as a state senator from Charleston, and in 1879 was elected a member of the U.S. Congress, where he spoke out on behalf of civil rights for black citizens.

In the first two decades after the war, black churches experienced explosive growth as the "invisible institution" took on visible form. Black preachers who had been ministering to their people for years under the supervision of whites rapidly formed black congregations, scattered across the South. And, in some cases, they resented the intrusion of their fellow black ministers from the North.

The freedom of association that Southern blacks finally could enjoy also enabled them to form hundreds of lodges, fraternal orders, and secret societies, with names like the Knights of Liberty, the Knights of Pythias, and the Knights and Daughters of Tabor. Most of these included insurance and mutual aid to assist members in times of sickness and to pay for burial expenses. The Prince Hall Masons, a fraternal society founded in Boston in 1775 by a free black named Prince Hall, also established chapters in the South. (The Freemasons were an international secret fraternal order dedicated to principles of brotherhood, charity, and mutual assistance to members. In the United States the establishment of a separate black Masonic order became necessary because white Masons refused to admit black men.) Besides mutual aid, these fraternal organizations created opportunities for fellowship and for the public celebration of black citizenship in parades, ceremonies, and speeches. Sometimes black ministers criticized secret societies for taking money and energy away from the churches, but in many cases the leadership of church and lodge actually overlapped.

A group of Masons gather to lay a cornerstone for a temple in Brooklyn in 1922. The Masons and other black societies offered mutual-aid assistance and insurance, as well as supporting social and civic activities.

Most of the black churches built after the war by former slaves were modest structures at best. Many congregations could afford nothing more for their house of worship than a brush arbor, a small wooden praise (or prayer) house or remodeled shed. They saved their meager funds, raised money from church suppers and donations, and gradually built simple wood-frame churches. There they worshiped as their parents and grandparents had, continuing to seek and find solace and hope as equality failed to follow freedom and opportunity seemed to elude them. As the distance between African Americans and the institution of slavery widened, the church remained a source of continuity, as well as a source of adaptation to new and different circumstances.

The Civil War and the end of slavery had seemed to validate the slaves' belief in the promises of God, but the freed people discovered that racial oppression showed no signs of disappearing. Decades after emancipation, they still had not entered the Promised Land. The brief opening that Reconstruction gave to black men to vote and to participate in government ended as Southern whites seized power in state after state by means of intimidation, discrimination, and outright violence. The former slaves were effectively abandoned by the U.S. government in 1877, when the last federal troops left the South.

Without federal protection, Southern blacks had no recourse under a system of laws enforced by local white supremacists intent on driving them out of politics. Gradually deprived of the vote, black Southerners found themselves increasingly segregated in public places, forced into second-class schools, and denied access to other civic institutions. They saw their legal challenge to the spread of Jim Crow (a term for segregation derived from a 19th-century minstrel song that made fun of black people) denied by the U.S. Supreme Court in the *Plessy v. Ferguson* decision of 1896, which upheld the legality of segregation using the principle of "separate but equal"; that is, it was all right to have separate facilities for whites and blacks as long as they provided equal services.

New scientific and pseudo-scientific theories, from evolution to phrenology (measuring intellectual ability by the shape of the skull), claimed to prove that black people were innately inferior to whites.

Old racial stereotypes in books, newspapers, and popular entertainment portrayed the Negro as a beast to a new generation of Americans. Incidents of violence against African Americans became more frequent. Between 1882 and 1885, 227 black people were lynched. Between 1889 and 1899, that figure rose to 1,240. These lynchings took place mainly, but not exclusively, in the South. In 1898 alone, white mobs seized and murdered 104 black people.

Facing the bleak situation of blacks in the United States decades after slavery had ended, black ministers struggled to find some meaning, some message of hope while the situation of their people seemed in many ways to be worsening instead of improving. Discussions about the destiny of African Americans gravitated toward two major themes: "the Redemption of Africa" and "the Mission of the Darker Races," to use the terms of the times. The first idea maintained that the role of African Americans, as laid out in God's plan to save the world, was to "redeem Africa," that is, convert Africans to Christianity. Alexander Crummell, the chief black American proponent of missions to Africa in the latter part of the 19th century, reminded African Americans of their duty to transmit Western civilization and the Christian gospel to Africans. A cousin of Henry Highland Garnet, he himself had been a missionary to Liberia for 20 years. It was the proper mission of the black American, he said, to bring the gospel to the African. Whites had no business in Africa. As the Baptist minister Emmanuel K. Love stated before the Black Baptist Foreign Mission Convention in 1889, "There is no doubt in my mind that Africa is our field of operation and that [as] Moses was sent to deliver his brethren, and as the prophets were members of the race to whom they were sent, so I am convinced that God's purpose is to redeem Africa through us. This work is ours by appointment, by inheritance, and by choice." Europeans had failed in their previous attempts to Christianize Africa, but African Americans would succeed because their race would arouse Africans' confidence, not their distrust.

A few blacks, including a number of women, heeded the call to go to Africa as missionaries in the late 19th century. One of the most interesting of these was Maria Fearing. Born in 1838 to slave parents in

Alexander Crummell, a cousin of Henry Highland Garnet and an Episcopalian priest, served as a missionary in Liberia for 20 years. He argued forcefully for sending African-American missionaries to Africa in the late 19th century.

Gainesville, Alabama, Fearing was 27 years old when emancipation came. She began her formal education at the age of 33, completing the ninth grade at Talladega College. Then she taught for a while in a rural school in Alabama before returning to Talladega as an assistant matron. In 1894, William Sheppard, a black missionary on leave from the Congo, lectured at Talladega on the African missions and the need for black American missionaries to take up the task.

At the age of 56, Fearing decided to become a missionary. No missionary board would support her because she was thought to be too old, so she sold her home, took her life's savings, and joined Sheppard's return party to the Congo in 1894. There she began to learn the languages of the local people and worked among the women and children. She sheltered orphaned and kidnapped girls and built a home for girls that she managed until 1915, when she retired and returned home at the age of 77.

The interest of black American churches in Africa sometimes helped in the development of independent African churches. In 1892, African members of the Wesleyan Methodist Church in the Transvaal (later part of South Africa) withdrew to establish their own "Ethiopian Church." Its pastor, the Reverend Mangena Maake Mokone, learned of the history of the African Methodist Episcopal Church in 1895 and wrote to Bishop Henry McNeal Turner to ask for assistance in educating South African students and for advice on developing his Ethiopian Church. After a series of letters between the two men, the Ethiopian Church conference voted to affiliate with the AME Church and sent the Reverend James Dwane to the United States to complete the merger. Turner remarked that the South Africans were as justified in breaking with the white Methodists as Richard Allen had been a century earlier.

In 1896 the Ethiopian Church of Transvaal became the 14th District of the AME Church, and in 1898 Turner traveled to South Africa to ordain 31 elders and 20 deacons. (Deacon and elder were the two levels of ordination within the AME Church.) In 1901 Bishop Levi J. Coppin arrived in Cape Town as the first resident bishop of the AME Church in Africa. More Africans began to travel to the United States to study in black seminaries

People gather in front of the main building of Howard University in Washington, D.C. Founded in 1867, the university is still flourishing.

and colleges, including Lynchburg Baptist Seminary in Virginia, Lincoln University in Pennsylvania, and Howard University in Washington, D.C.

Black churches, however, lacked the funds to support more than a few missionaries to Africa, and attempts to work through the missionary boards of white denominations yielded only small numbers. Nevertheless, the challenge of African missions loomed large in the consciousness of black Christians. Africa stood for opportunity and equal rights; the United States for discrimination and oppression. Symbolically, the mission to redeem Africa confirmed the importance of African Americans as a people. The power of this idea was reflected in the logo of the AME journal, the *Christian Recorder,* redesigned in 1869. The plain title in bold type was replaced by a picture of the globe, turned to the continent of Africa. Three sailing ships from the United States drew near the coasts of Africa. Rays of light shot out from the "dark continent" and beneath the globe stretched a banner proclaiming: "Ethiopia shall soon stretch forth her hands to God"— a graphic restatement of African-American destiny, the redemption of Africa.

Some African Americans felt that emigrating to Africa was the only escape from the racism that surrounded them in the United States. According to AME bishop Henry McNeal Turner, the mission to Africa offered black Americans the opportunity to assert their rights without the limitations of U.S. segregation and racism. Turner urged blacks to reject racism, to respect themselves and other black people, and argued that they ought to imagine and depict God in their own image just as whites did—a black God for black people.

"The Mission of the Darker Races," the second major theme debated by black clergy, was sparked by theological reflection upon the experience of racial oppression in the United States in the late 19th century. This interpretation of black destiny asserted that it was the mission of African Americans to save Christianity in the United States from racism, militarism, and materialism. Europeans and European Americans, they said, had turned Christianity into an ethnocentric (racially prejudiced) "clan religion." They had become too corrupt to preach the true gospel to the non-Christian peoples of the world. Two black theologians, Theophilus Gould Steward, an AME minister, and James Theodore Holly, an Episcopalian bishop, predicted that Western civilization was finished, and that other peoples, "the darker races of the world," would at last put into practice the gospel that white Christians had only preached. People who thought along these lines acted upon their beliefs by fighting actively against discrimination, lynching, and other manifestations of white oppression in the United States.

Black clergymen were joined in this protest by black churchwomen, who organized women's auxiliaries to the male-controlled denominational boards and spoke out boldly on a variety of issues. For example, black Baptist women organized state conventions beginning in the 1880s, and in 1900 more than a million members attended the first national Women's Convention, an auxiliary to the National Baptist Convention. Under the leadership of S. Willie Layten of Philadelphia, Nannie Burroughs of Philadelphia, and Virginia Broughton of Nashville, the Women's Convention urged black mothers to teach their children the moral virtues necessary for the progress of the race. The convention also

Black Americans Protest Lynching

Born a slave at Holly Springs, Mississippi, in 1862, Ida B. Wells attended nearby Rust College, edited and wrote for black newspapers in Memphis and Chicago, and launched an activist career as a critic of racial injustice that lasted until her death in 1931. In 1898, Wells went to the White House with a delegation of congressmen from Illinois to appeal personally to President William McKinley to stop the lynching of blacks. She petitioned:

Mr. President, the colored citizens of this country . . . desire to respectfully urge that some action be taken by you as chief magistrate of this great nation . . . we most earnestly desire that national legislation be enacted for the suppression of the national crime of lynching. For nearly 20 years lynching crimes . . . have been committed and permitted by this Christian nation. Nowhere in the civilized world save the United States do men, possessing all civil and political power, go out in bands of 50 to 5,000 to hunt down, shoot, hang or burn to death a single individual, unarmed and absolutely powerless. Statistics show that nearly 10,000 American citizens have been lynched in the past 20 years. To our appeals for justice the stereotyped reply has been that the government could not interfere in a state matter. . . . We refuse to believe this country, so powerful to defend its citizens abroad . . . is unable to protect its citizens at home.

Nannie Helen Burroughs—
educator, civil rights
advocate, and religious
leader—founded the
National Training School
for Women and Girls in
Washington, D.C. in 1909.

demanded for all black people equal treatment on public transportation, the right to vote in every state of the country, equal treatment in the courts, equal amounts of school funds, an end to lynching, and better treatment of blacks in prisons. Black women church leaders also cooperated with white women church leaders to bring about social reform at a time when interracial cooperation was rare. The national club movement among black women also owed a great deal to the black churches, where its leaders and members learned their organizational skills.

Black responses to segregation and racism in the United States were still largely formulated through the church, but two nonclerical figures, Booker T. Washington and W.E.B. DuBois, dominated the discussion of race in this period. The two men had opposite responses to the racial situation. Washington advocated industrial education as the most realistic path to progress for a largely rural people. DuBois, a Harvard-educated scholar and social activist, stressed the need for liberal education to train an intellectual elite to lead an uneducated people. Washington emphasized black economic development and advised patience concerning social equality between the races (even as he secretly funded legal challenges to segregation). DuBois encouraged protest for black civil rights and argued that black economic advancement depended upon the political and legal protection guaranteed by blacks being able to vote. Washington and DuBois each had their supporters among the clergy.

The disagreement between DuBois and Washington reveals a sometimes overlooked fact: African-American opinion has never been unanimous. The various perspectives of African Americans on social issues in the 19th century reflected their differences in class, education, residence, and religion.

All of these differing opinions became more accessible to the public as the black press expanded in the late 19th century. Newspapers, journals, and books expressed the thoughts of African Americans on a variety of issues, including religious controversies. There was much debate at that time about scientific discoveries that seemed to contradict a literal interpretation of the Bible, and the black press circulated and publicized interpretations of Scripture, theology, and history by black authors, both clergy and laymen. And journals such as the *AME Church Review* pub-

When Fisk College, one of the country's most Important black institutions, faced financial problems in 1871, a group of students known as the Fisk Jubilee Singers staged a series of concerts that introduced traditional black spirituals to audiences around the world. Their tour was a success, and Fisk remained open.

lished poems, short stories, essays, book reviews, and sketches of prominent black Americans.

Black culture entered a new phase of self-reflection, as the folkways of the slaves began to be either criticized as outdated and superstitious or celebrated as heroic and noble. The Fisk Jubilee Singers, a group of male and female students from Fisk College, performed concerts of spirituals before enthusiastic audiences in England and Europe. They raised thousands of dollars for their school and introduced the spirituality of African-American slaves to the world. By contrast, the rise of blues music gave voice to a secular counterpart to the religious culture of black Americans, revealing that many black Americans did not belong to churches or live by their rules of conduct.

Church membership is a concrete measure of the influence of religion upon a people's life. In 1890, the black population of the United States totaled 8.3 million people; of that number, 2.7 million, about 33 percent, were church members. By this standard, black churches had attained an amazing level of growth in the 40 years since emancipation, and in the midst of rapid change they would continue to shape the thought, politics, and culture of African Americans in the 20th century.

Chapter 5

From Plantation to Ghetto: Religion in the City

n 1890, 90 percent of the African-American population was concentrated in the South. Between 1890 and 1930 more than 2.5 million black people left the South, and increasing numbers of those who remained moved from the country to the city. By 1930, 44 percent of the black population lived in the urban areas of the nation. What caused this massive movement? The main two factors that pushed rural black farmers off the land were a depressed rural economy and racial discrimination. In the 1890s, a series of natural disasters, including boll weevil infestations, ruined the cotton crop, the main staple of Southern farming, and produced economic misery for black sharecroppers and tenant farmers. In addition, the pervasive system of racial discrimination and the threat of violence against any black person who stood up to the system hindered the efforts of black Southerners to better their condition. The factors that pulled them toward the cities included the expansion of industrial jobs in the North and the shortage of cheap labor due to the outbreak of World War I in 1914, which reduced the supply of unskilled laborers from Europe. Industries in large cities sent labor agents into the South to recruit black workers. The black press, especially the *Chicago Defender,* advertised the opportunities and freedoms available for blacks in the North.

In 1915 and 1916, boll weevils again ruined the cotton crop over an extensive area of the South, devastating the income of thousands of black

Black migrants from the South flocked to large urban churches like the Victory Tabernacle after they moved north. Many churches helped them find jobs and education.

tenant farmers and sharecroppers. As a result, 500,000 black people moved North. Letters from migrants described how much better the North was and encouraged their families and friends to follow. Patterns of settlement in the cities depended on geography and railroad lines, so that people from Mississippi, for example, tended to settle in Chicago. In some cases the majority of a Southern church community moved North and were later joined by their pastor. Particular church congregations in Northern and Western cities consisted mainly of migrants from one area of the South.

The urban situation turned out to be less rosy than the migrants had hoped. As they settled into the poorer sections of the cities, they encountered conflict with white neighbors and white workers, frequently of immigrant background. Friction over competition for jobs, availability of housing, and the exclusion of blacks from labor unions, as well as the use of black workers to break strikes, led to anger and resentment on the part of working-class whites. Race riots broke out in Philadelphia and East St. Louis in 1917. Economic recession after the war produced mass layoffs of black workers in an application of the "last hired, first fired" policy. Black soldiers returned from service in World War I, where they had fought in segregated all-black units to "make the world safe for democracy," as President Woodrow Wilson had put it. Some of them had served under black officers, had seen combat against the Germans, and had been treated as equals by their French allies. In contrast, white American soldiers persisted in viewing black servicemen as inferior. Having fought for their country, African-American veterans felt that they had proved on the battlefield that blacks were equal to whites, and they demanded an end to discrimination at home. Their militance angered some whites, and mobs in the South attacked and beat black servicemen and stripped them of their uniforms. The segregation of federal employees in Washington, D.C., and the 1915 revival of the Ku Klux Klan (a secret society violently opposed to racial equality) as a national organization demonstrated to blacks the persistance of racism at all levels of society and in all parts of the country.

The "great migration" had begun and would continue until the 1950s. This massive movement of people disrupted rural and urban congregations, transplanted Southern religious customs North and West, strained the resources of urban churches, and formed in black city neighborhoods new opportunities for religious creativity. Facing an unfamiliar urban environment, country-raised migrants looked to the churches to reaffirm the traditional values and community ties that had always given them a sense of social location back home. In some instances they joined already-established churches; in others they founded new ones of their own. The sheer numbers of migrants enlarged the membership of existing churches and tested their capacity to absorb the new arrivals. In the early years of the migration, some churches were so overcrowded that they had to hold double services on Sundays. As the migrants continued to flood in by the thousands, pastors and church boards started extensive and expensive construction projects to increase the seating capacity of

At the height of its power, the Ku Klux Klan marched down Pennsylvania Avenue in Washington, D.C., in 1926. Klan members attempted to terrorize blacks and to preserve white supremacy.

Members of St. Phillip's Episcopal Church in Harlem belonged to a church that took an active role in housing and health care in the local community.

their buildings. Some churches acted as welfare agencies, organizing for community service. For example, Abyssinian Baptist Church in New York, Olivet Baptist in Chicago, and First Congregational in Atlanta ran employment bureaus, day-care centers, kindergartens, adult education classes, drama groups, orchestras, social clubs, athletic events, outreach clubs, and various youth programs. In the 1920s Olivet Baptist, led by Lacey Kirk Williams, had 42 departments and auxiliaries, 512 officers, 23 salaried workers, a congregation of 8,743 members, a Sunday School enrollment of 3,100, two buildings, and five assistant pastors.

While some of the newcomers took pride in the size and prestige of the large city churches, others missed the intimacy and the recognition they had enjoyed in the small churches "down home." Differences in levels of education and income and in styles of worship distinguished some migrants from some longtime residents, as well as from each other. The emotionalism and spontaneity of many rural Southern services clashed with the proper decorum of urban Northern churches. These differences, as well as the usual divisiveness of church politics, splintered congregations and multiplied the number of churches in urban black neighborhoods. Many of these congregations were so poor and so small that they gathered in storefronts or private homes for worship. Some newly formed churches, called missions, managed to grow and eventually purchase or construct a church building. Others remained in storefronts.

Besides increasing the size and number of urban black churches, migration also increased the variety of black religious life by exposing people to new religious choices. Accustomed to deciding between Baptist,

Methodist, and perhaps Holiness-Pentecostal churches back home, migrants to the cities encountered black Jews, black Muslims, black Catholics, black Spiritualists (people who believed that the living could communicate with the dead), and black disciples of charismatic religious figures like Daddy Grace, the founder of a church called the Universal House of Prayer for All People, who believed that their leaders could exercise divine power to heal their problems in this world as well as the next.

The most famous figure of the period, however, was not apparently a religious leader, although there were religious aspects to his movement, which was the largest mass movement ever organized among African Americans. That man was Marcus Mosiah Garvey, the founder of an organization called the Universal Negro Improvement Association.

Garvey was born in Jamaica in 1887. As a young man he learned the trade of printing and began publishing his own newspaper in 1910. He traveled in Central America and relocated in 1912 to England, where he worked on the *African Times and Orient Review* and learned the philosophy of Pan-Africanism, an intellectual and political movement that preached racial pride and unity, "Africa for Africans," and the formation of an African national homeland for the dispersed peoples of African descent. He read Booker T. Washington's autobiography, *Up From Slavery,* and decided to meet Washington in order to convince him to establish a trade school to train black Americans to go to Africa as "technical missionaries."

In 1914 Garvey left London for Jamaica and organized the Universal Negro Improvement Association and African Communities League (UNIA) for the purpose of "uniting all the Negro peoples of the world into one great body to establish a country and Government absolutely of their own." He received an invitation to visit the United States from Booker T. Washington, but he arrived in 1916 only to discover that Washington had died. Deciding to stay in the United States, Garvey lectured and organized a branch of his organization, which mushroomed rapidly to 2,000 members, in New York City. He started publishing a journal, *The Negro World,* to spread news of Pan-Africanism and his own ideas. Garvey's movement spread everywhere black communities existed. The UNIA was

Marcus Garvey led the largest mass movement in black American history, the Universal Negro Improvement Association. Garvey taught race pride, self-help, and the solidarity of black people around the world.

a multipurpose organization, serving political, social, cultural, economic, and religious needs. Garveyites met in buildings called Liberty Halls and held a variety of programs, including Sunday morning services, afternoon Sunday schools, public meetings, dances, and concerts. The halls offered temporary housing, soup kitchens, and jobs for the unemployed.

The UNIA had its own flag, its own national anthem, and its own steamship line, all to create a sense of national belonging among its members, who felt alienated from the United States. For those alienated from a white version of Christianity, the UNIA supplied a weekly Sunday service, a baptismal ritual, a hymnal, a creed, a catechism, the image of Jesus Christ as a "Black Man of Sorrows" and the Virgin Mary as a "Black Madonna." The creed proclaimed in part, "We believe in God, the Creator of all things and people, in Jesus Christ, His Son, the Spiritual Savior of all mankind. We believe in Marcus Garvey, the leader of the Negro peoples of the world, and in the program enunciated by him through the UNIA." The *Universal Negro Catechism* (1921), arranged in question and answer format similar to the traditional Catholic catechism, provided ammunition to defend against anti-black ideas, such as the old notion that Noah's curse of Ham in the book of Genesis justified the enslavement of Africans (the supposed descendants of Ham):

Q. Is it true that Noah cursed his son Ham?
A. No; he cursed Canaan, the youngest son of Ham . . .

Q. Who are the descendants of Canaan?
A. The Caananites who dwelt in Palestine before the Jews took possession of it.

Q. Are Negroes concerned in this curse of Noah?
A. Certainly not. . . .

Q. What prediction made in the 68th Psalm and the 31st verse is now being fulfilled?

A. "Princes shall come out of Egypt, Ethiopia shall soon stretch out her hands unto God."

Q. What does this verse prove?

A. That Black Men will set up their own government in Africa, with rulers of their own race.

The UNIA's two slogans, "Up you mighty race" and "One God, One Aim, One Destiny" spread the message of black pride and solidarity among peoples of African descent. UNIA-sponsored parades, with full dress uniforms and banners, demonstrated to spectators the ideals of black identity and independence. Garvey and his movement aroused opposition from other black leaders and the suspicion of the Federal Bureau of Investigation, which decided that Garvey posed a threat to national security. He was arrested, tried for mail fraud, and found guilty. After serving two years in prison, he was deported in 1927. Without his leadership the UNIA fell apart as an organization, but Garvey's ideals of racial unity and Pan-African liberation had a profound impact upon black Americans, influenced independence movements in Africa and the West Indies, and led diverse groups such as the Rastafarians (Jamaicans who believed in the divinity of the Ethiopian ruler Haile Selassie) and the Black Muslims to regard him as a prophet. (One of Garvey's supporters, in fact, was the Reverend Earl Little, a Baptist minister and the father of future Black Muslim leader Malcolm X.)

While Garvey encouraged African Americans to embrace their racial identity, other leaders claimed that they had discovered the authentic identity of black people that had been taken from them by the experience of slavery. Since the days of slavery, black Americans had identified themselves symbolically with the biblical Israelites. The first organization to take this identification literally was the Church of God and Saints of Christ, founded in 1896 by William S. Crowdy in Lawrence, Kansas. Crowdy preached that black people descended from the 10 lost tribes of Israel.

Similar beliefs inspired the development of several black Jewish congregations in New York. In the 1920s, Wentworth A. Matthew formed the Commandment Keepers Congregation of the Living God, for years Harlem's largest congregation of black Jews. The Commandment Keepers believed that African Americans were "Ethiopian Hebrews" who had been robbed of their true religion by slavery. Judaism was the ancestral heritage of the Ethiopians, whereas Christianity was the religion of the "Gentiles," that is, whites. Many of these early black Jewish congregations combined Jewish and Christian customs in their services and observances, reading, for example, from the Christian New Testament as well as the Hebrew Bible.

The first organized movement of black Americans to identify itself as Muslim (as distinct from Muslim individuals and families during slavery) was founded by a railroad worker from North Carolina named Timothy Drew. In 1913, the Noble Drew Ali, as his followers called him, established the first Moorish Science Temple in Newark, New Jersey. Ali claimed that African Americans were not Negroes but "Asiatics." Their original homeland was Morocco; their true nationality was Moorish American. To symbolize the recovery of their true identity, those who joined the Moorish Science Temple received new names and identity cards issued by Noble Drew Ali. Knowledge of their true selves, Ali taught, would empower them to overcome racism.

The doctrines of Moorish Science were explained in "The Holy Koran," a 60-page booklet of beliefs and doctrines that bore no resemblance to the Koran of Islam. The Moorish Science text declared that just as John the Baptist was the forerunner of Jesus, so Marcus Garvey was the forerunner of the Noble Drew Ali, "who was prepared and sent to this earth to teach the old-time religion and the everlasting gospel to the sons of men." By 1925, Ali had founded several temples and moved his headquarters to Chicago. The Moorish Science Temple continued after Ali's death in 1929, but was overshadowed by another black Muslim group that received much more national attention.

In 1930, a man named Wallace D. Fard began teaching poor blacks in Detroit that they were members of a Muslim "lost-found tribe of Shabazz," and that salvation for black people depended upon "knowledge of self." In 1933 Fard was arrested for disturbing the peace. Ordered by the police to leave Detroit, he left his followers under the care of his chief assistant, Elijah Poole, whose name he changed to Elijah Muhammad. Elijah Muhammad guided the movement for the next 40 years.

The organization, which Fard named the Nation of Islam, grew from two small congregations in Detroit and Chicago to dozens of mosques with thousands of members in every section of the country. Elijah Muhammad taught that Master Fard had actually been the incarnation of Allah, and that he, Elijah, was his messenger. His message included an elaborate account of human origins in which humankind was originally black until an evil scientist experimenting with genes created a race of white people. The whites he created turned out to be devils. Their religion is Christianity, whereas that of the original black people is Islam. Allah has allowed the race of white devils to rule the world for 6000 years, a period that would soon end in the destruction of the world, after which a new one would be ruled by the black Nation. Instead of striving for integration, therefore, blacks should separate themselves from the corrupt, doomed white society.

Although these beliefs were heretical in the eyes of orthodox Muslims, to Messenger Elijah's followers they seemed a plausible explanation for white racism and an effective antidote to the myth of white supremacy and black inferiority. Elijah Muhammad proposed a detailed program for the Nation that included establishing black Muslim businesses in order to gain economic independence and a demand that the federal government set aside separate land for African Americans in reparation for slavery. The separate identity of members of the Nation was reinforced by a strict ethical code. Alcohol, drugs, tobacco, movies, sports, and cosmetics were forbidden, along with pork and other foods identified as unclean or unhealthy. Though differing drastically from the religion of worldwide Islam, the Moorish Science Temple and the Nation of Islam spread awareness of Islam as an alternative to Christianity among black Americans.

By rejecting Christianity as a religion of whites and by denying that American racial categories applied to them, black Jews and black Muslims created new racial, national, and religious identities for themselves. They believed that these ancient worldwide religious communities made no racial distinctions and they felt that within the temple or the mosque they could avoid the racial hypocrisy of Christianity as practiced in the United States.

While black Muslims and Jews preached non-Christian religious identities for African Americans, black Catholics appealed to the universal, raceless character of Christianity as the solution to the problem of racism in America. As rural Southern blacks migrated to Northern cities, they encountered black Catholics who had migrated from Louisiana or Maryland and white Catholics of European immigrant background. Some black Protestants decided that Catholic parochial schools offered their children a better education than public schools. Over the years, parochial schools became an important source of black converts to Roman Catholicism.

The number of black priests, however, remained very small. The first black priests, James, Patrick, and Alexander Healy, were followed by Augustus Tolton. Born a slave in Missouri, Tolton, like the Healys, had to go abroad to seek seminary training. Ordained in Rome in 1886, he founded a parish for black Catholics in Chicago. Tolton was acclaimed by black Protestants, as well as Catholics, as "our Colored Priest." In 1891, more than a century after the first black Baptist and Methodist clergy had emerged to minister to their people, Charles Randolph Uncles was ordained by Cardinal James Gibbons in Baltimore, becoming the first black priest to be ordained in this country. In 1920 St. Augustine's Seminary was established by the Society of the Divine Word in Bay St. Louis, Mississippi, specifically to train black men for the priesthood, as they were still unwelcome in the seminaries of most dioceses and religious orders.

In the absence of black priests, black laypeople took up the task of defining the meaning of Roman Catholicism for African Americans. From 1889 to 1894, delegates from around the country met in five annual congresses of black Catholics. They met to discuss common issues, to encourage education of black Catholic youth, and to protest discrimination within the church.

The organizer of these congresses was Daniel A. Rudd, a descendant of Catholic slaves from Kentucky. Rudd, a journalist by profession, edited a black Catholic newspaper, the *American Catholic Tribune* (1887–1895), first published in Springfield, Ohio, then Cincinnati, Ohio, and finally in Detroit, Michigan. In the pages of the nationally distributed *Tribune,* Rudd argued that salvation for African Americans lay not in Protestantism, with its separate "race" churches, but in the universalism of the Roman Catholic church. With its history of accepting all races and of including Africans like St. Monica, St. Augustine, St. Cyprian, St. Moses, and St. Benedict the Moor among its calendar of canonized saints, the Roman Catholic Church proved that it did not discriminate by race. While praising the openness of Catholicism to all races, the delegates to the black congresses criticized the exclusion of black children over 12 years of age from Catholic schools, appointed a committee to gather reports of discrimination, and reported their findings to the Vatican in Rome.

Increasing numbers of rural black migrants from the South converted to the Roman Catholicism of the northern cities when they went north. Augustus Tolton, born a slave, was ordained a priest in 1886 and worked among black Catholics in Chicago until his death in 1897.

The activism of Rudd and the black Catholic congresses was continued in the 20th century by the Federated Colored Catholics, founded in 1917 by Dr. Thomas Wyatt Turner, a descendant of Catholic slaves from southern Maryland and a professor of biology, first at Howard University and then at the Hampton Institute. The Federated Colored Catholics organized black Catholics nationally, developed black leadership locally, and protested racial prejudice within and without the church until the mid-1950s.

In 1891, a new order of nuns, the Sisters of the Blessed Sacrament for Indians and Colored People, founded by Katherine Drexel to educate African Americans and Native Americans, joined with the Josephite Fathers, an order of men founded in England in 1866, in taking on a particular mission to black Americans. Katherine Drexel, born in Philadelphia in 1858, was heir to the fortune of her father, wealthy

Congresses of black Catholics met five times in the late 19th century to discuss their common concerns and to protest discrimination within the Catholic Church.

Philadelphia banker Francis Anthony Drexel. As the Mother Superior (spiritual and administrative supervisor) of the Sisters of the Blessed Sacrament, Mother Katherine gave financial support to numerous missions, churches, and schools throughout the South and the Southwest. In 1915, she laid the foundation for a school in New Orleans that became Xavier University of Louisiana, thus providing black Catholics with an institution of higher education.

One of the most significant of the religious movements to attract blacks during the period of migration was in many ways a return to the emphasis on spiritual experience and emotional worship of the "old-time" religion. In the late 19th century, an interdenominational movement that stressed the ideal of holiness emerged out of the Methodist and several other churches. The proponents of this Holiness movement preached that there was a second spiritual experience after conversion, called sanctification, which made the Christian holy. In 1885, two black Baptist ministers, Charles H. Mason and Charles P. Jones, accepted the Holiness doctrine of sanctification and began to preach it to Baptist congregations in Mississippi. Expelled by the local Baptist association, they proceeded in 1897 to organize the Church of God in Christ in Memphis, Tennessee.

About the same time, some advocates of Holiness began to speak of still another experience beyond sanctification, called baptism with the Spirit, an experience of the presence of the Holy Spirit received as a gift from God. Under the power of the Spirit, these 20th-century Christians expected to speak in unknown tongues just as the disciples of Jesus did on the feast of Pentecost (a religious festival held 50 days after Passover) as recorded in the Acts of the Apostles. Hence the name for this new movement—Pentecostalism. Along with speaking in tongues, the other gifts of the Spirit included prophesy, the ability to predict or reveal the meaning of events; healing, the ability to cure physical and emotional illness by prayer and (usually) by touch; interpretation, the ability to translate and explain the meaning of what is spoken in unknown tongues; and judgment (or distinguishing) of spirits, the ability to determine if a prophecy or other spiritual gift is authentically from God.

In 1906, William J. Seymour, a black Holiness preacher, started a prayer meeting in a private home in Los Angeles. As people began speaking in tongues, the crowd increased and a religious revival began that quickly outgrew the house. The revivalists quickly relocated to an old building on Azusa Street in downtown Los Angeles. For the next three years the Azusa Street Revival attracted white, black, Hispanic, and Asian Christians from all over the nation—indeed from around the world—eager to receive baptism with the Spirit and the gift of speaking in tongues. Among the thousands of pilgrims who flocked to Azusa Street was Charles H. Mason, who received the gift of Spirit baptism. When Mason returned to Memphis in 1907 and preached the doctrine of speaking in tongues, his colleague Charles Jones rejected the new message and a split in the church developed. The majority of members followed Mason into the Pentecostal movement, and they kept the name the Church of God in Christ. Under the leadership of Mason, the Church of God in Christ became the largest black Penetecostal denomination. Jones and his group took the name Church of Christ (Holiness) U.S.A. The "sanctified" churches, as the Holiness and Pentecostal congregations were called, encouraged their

Father Divine greets his followers during a parade in Harlem celebrating his newest "heaven" community.

members to express the gifts of the Spirit. They also required that their members abstain from tobacco, alcohol, drugs, gambling, dancing, makeup, and "worldly" entertainment, such as concerts, movies, and theater. Ridiculed by outsiders as "holy rollers" because of the emotional expressiveness of their services, they introduced the use of "secular" musical instruments such as guitars, pianos, and drums into their religious services, and made a major contribution to the development of black gospel music. Their style of religious music eventually influenced the tastes of churches that once banned such instruments as tools of the devil.

In effect, the congregations created little social worlds within the larger, often hostile white world. Members were trained to develop habits of honesty, thrift, hard work, and discipline. Eventually they tended to move up economically and educationally, within the limits set by racial discrimination.

At its beginnings the Pentecostal movement had inspired interracial cooperation. The leadership of the Azusa Street Revival included whites as well as blacks, and Mason ordained many white Pentecostal ministers. But by 1920, sanctified churches, like the larger society in the United States, had split along racial lines. A century after the Methodist and Baptist movements had tried and failed, the Holiness and Pentecostal movements were no more successful at sustaining interracial Christian community in the face of widespread racial prejudice, discrimination, and segregation.

A wide range of new religious options confronted African Americans in the urban world, including religious communities that gathered around new messiahs. In the 1930s and 1940s the best-known nationally was Father Divine (1879–1965), who was believed by his followers to have the power to heal illness, poverty, and racism. George Baker, Jr., as he was known before taking the name Father Divine, was born in Rockville, Maryland. As a young man he moved to Baltimore, where he worked as a gardener and developed an interest in religious ideas, including the theory that negative thinking produced illness and problems whereas positive thinking tapped into the power of God and produced healing. Baker began to preach his religious message on street corners and in private homes, slowly gathering a following.

In 1906 he visited the Azusa Street Revival and claimed to have received an experience of God's presence within himself. Continuing his traveling ministry, he began to teach that God, who had once become human in Jesus, had now become human again in a Negro, namely, himself. He moved to Brooklyn, New York, in 1917, and began to gather a small community of believers. That year he took the name Reverend Major Jealous (M.J.) Divine, suggesting perhaps his identity as the new incarnation of God. His followers simply addressed him as Father Divine. Numerous testimonies from converts claimed that the mention of his name or meditating upon his kindness had cured them of tuberculosis, heart trouble, paralysis, and other ailments. Father Divine taught his followers that illness and death resulted from failures in faith. If they simply thought about Father during times of trouble, their problems would disappear. The more closely they lived his teachings, the closer they came to being divine and immortal themselves. The followers of Father Divine avoided alcohol, tobacco, gambling, racial prejudice, and sexual intercourse.

As Father Divine's flock grew larger, he gained white as well as black converts and relocated his headquarters first to Sayville, Long Island, then to Harlem, New York. During the 1920s and 1930s he established communities called "heavens" in cities across the country. These heavens attracted numerous visitors because of their huge banquets, which were served even during the worst years of the Depression as visible proof of Father Divine's benevolence. His followers took the name Peace Mission Movement and campaigned for an end to segregation and racial hatred. His emphasis on salvation from disease, hunger, poverty, discrimination, and war in this world addressed the needs of those who were tired of waiting for happiness in some other world. Father Divine offered them salvation in the here and now.

The concentration of black population in the cities and the development of new communication and entertainment media like radio and the phonograph spread black religious culture to a wide audience. Record companies produced "race records" specifically designed for black listeners. These included blues and jazz music, as well as 700 sermons recorded between 1925 and 1941 by Baptist preachers A.W. Nix, J.C. Burnett, and J.M. Gates, and by Pentecostal preachers D.C. Rice and F.W. McGee, all accompanied by instrumental music and congregational singing. Radio stations featured black religious services or broadcast black preachers regularly to local listeners. Sheet music of gospel songs was published and sold to black choirs. At first, the music was controversial, as some ministers and congregations condemned it for sounding too much like blues or the singing of the sanctified congregations they disdained. Gradually, the music became more acceptable as congregations experienced its spiritual power.

The career of one of the most influential composers of gospel, Thomas A. Dorsey, illustrates the evolution of gospel blues. Known as "Georgia Tom" when he toured the country with blues singer Ma Rainey from 1923 to 1926, Dorsey underwent a conversion experience that turned him from secular to sacred music. He began to write gospel songs and to travel widely, selling his music to local church choirs. Eventually he was hired as the music director of the influential Pilgrim Baptist Church in Chicago, where he was able to help develop gospel nationally by organizing an annual convention of gospel singers that brought together gospel choirs from around the country. "Precious Lord" and other Dorsey compositions were sung by generations of popular gospel soloists, many of them women such as Sallie Martin, Willie Mae Ford Smith, Marion Williams, and Mahalia Jackson. They understood themselves to be primarily evangelists, that is, preachers of the Gospel message through song. Gospel music had a major influence upon 20th-century black (and white) popular music, especially rhythm and blues. Many black singers and musicians owed their training to the music of the black churches.

Radio, records, and concerts also brought spirituals to whole new audiences. A succession of classical artists, including Roland Hayes, Paul Robeson, and Marian Anderson, featured renditions of the old slave songs in their concert tours around the world. And black literary figures celebrated the slaves' religious music as one of America's greatest contributions to world culture. For example, in his influential book of essays, *Souls of Black Folk,* published in 1903, W.E.B. DuBois argued that the poetic beauty and wisdom of the slaves' "sorrow songs" were equal to the best poetry of Europe. James Weldon Johnson, who was a novelist, teacher, U.S. consul to Venezuela and Nicaragua, and national secretary of the National Association for the Advancement of Colored People (NAACP), arranged two volumes of spirituals for modern performance and wrote a volume of poetry based upon the chanted sermon of the "old-time" black preacher, called *God's Trombones* (1927). DuBois also directed and published a sociological study called *Negro Church* in 1903, and Carter G. Woodson, founder of Negro (now African-American) History Month, wrote *History of the Negro Church* in 1921. These are just a few examples of works that demonstrate the growing scholarly interest in the importance of African-American religious institutions.

Marian Anderson, a classically trained contralto, included spirituals among the songs that she sang in concerts around the world.

Though the black population continued to become more urban with each passing decade, the rural churches remained the center of community life for African Americans who stayed on the land, and kept on influencing the religious attitudes and customs of those who migrated long after they had left for the city. In 1936, the number of rural black churches exceeded the number of urban ones 24,775 to 13,528. (However, urban church members outnumbered rural ones 2,958,630 to 2,701,988, reflecting the larger size of urban churches.)

Rural churches, like rural life, offered few creature comforts. Just to attend church meetings, people had to travel miles by foot, by mule, or by wagon over dusty, muddy, or snowy roads until the coming of paved roads and automobiles made traveling easier. The churches themselves were typically small frame structures of unpainted or whitewashed wood. Inside, rows of plain wooden benches faced a raised platform on which a pulpit and several chairs were set. Open windows and hand-held fans provided cool air in summer; wood-burning stoves radiated heat in winter. Before electricity, light was provided by kerosene or coal oil lamps.

The large majority of the membership was comprised of sharecroppers and tenant farmers, who paid rent to farm land owned by someone else. They did not have enough money to support a full-time pastor. As a result, many rural ministers served several congregations on alternate Sundays and earned their living by doing other kinds of work during the week.

Country preachers had less education than ministers in urban areas. Efforts to upgrade the education of rural ministers were sponsored during the 1930s and 1940s by home mission councils and educational organizations. Summer institutes for ministers met annually for one- or two-week sessions at Hampton Institute and Tuskegee Institute. Part-time classes and extension schools for ministers were conducted at several black colleges. In the minds of rural preachers and their congregations, though, education was secondary to the ability of the minister to preach. Even educated preachers were expected to preach in the spontaneous style of the chanted sermon.

But church was more than the minister and his sermon. It also involved the active participation of the people in the roles of deacons, ushers, choirs, song leaders, Sunday-school teachers, and "mothers" (the wise elders and advisors) of the church, as well as in a host of activities. These included leading prayers and hymns, reading Scripture, collecting the offering, hosting visitors, reporting spiritual experiences, and observing the customs and behavior that as children they had learned to associate with church.

As a result, the church instilled in its members an intimate sense of place, of being comfortably at home, and an experience of rootedness that stirred the memories of people who had moved away whenever they thought of "down home." The lasting attachment of migrants to their home church was celebrated annually on Homecoming, a day of special welcome to former members who had moved elsewhere. Sometimes the bodies of deceased former members were shipped back home, to the church of their baptism and the gravesite of their families, even though they had been members of another church for many years.

In the church, the sharecropper might hold the dignified office of deacon. There too, the young child might earn the applause of her elders

by reciting a poem on Children's Day. In church, 14- and 15-year-olds spoke movingly of their conversion experiences in front of the entire congregation. The church resembled an extended family, with which one shared the most important experiences of life. The decision of millions to leave the country for the city disrupted rural church congregations, and yet the migrants also carried rural Southern religious culture with them to every section of the country.

During the early decades of the 20th century, many of the black congregations of the South continued the religious traditions that had developed in slavery—the praise meeting, the revival, the mourner's bench, the conversion experience, and the emotionally charged preaching, singing, and shouting of worship services. These traditions helped poor black people to hold onto a sense of value and a degree of hope in a bleak social setting of discrimination, segregation, and racial violence. Out of these churches would come religious and moral resources, as well as the popular and institutional support for the development of the civil rights movement in the 1950s.

The rural black church, in spite of migration, remained the "down home" bedrock of black religious culture. This preacher stands before his congregation with his deacons during a revival meeting in La Forge, Missouri, in 1938.

103

Chapter 6

The Black Freedom Struggle

Studies of the black church written in the 1930s and 1940s by black scholars and social reformers, some of them ministers themseves, criticized the churches for failing to devote more energy to social and economic issues. Many black ministers, they claimed, were reluctant to attack discrimination and preached more about heaven and hell than about the problems troubling their people here on earth. Too many black ministers were poorly educated and ill-prepared to deal with modern change. And the growing number of black churches in the cities divided the black community into competing social clubs. If the churches had overcome their differences, the critics noted, they might have combined their resources and become an effective force for uplifting the race. Later historians, influenced by these critics, concluded that progressive black leadership had shifted in this period from the churches to secular organizations like the National Association for the Advancement of Colored People (NAACP) and the Urban League, which pursued equal rights for black people by taking legal action in the courts.

Although there was truth to these criticisms, black churches were more political and black protest more religious than the critics admitted. Black ministers were involved in the organization and growth of the NAACP, the Urban League, and Marcus Garvey's Universal Negro Improvement Association (UNIA). Northern and Southern black clergy

Protestant, Catholic, and Jewish clergy and laypeople gathered together at a civil rights rally in Selma, Alabama, to listen to the Reverend Andrew Young.

Marcus Garvey (in center, with sash) reviews members of the UNIA in a parade in New York City in 1924.

played active roles in movements for cooperation among the races long before the civil rights struggle of the 1950s and 1960s began. George Edmund Haynes, a black Congregationalist churchman, helped to found the Urban League and served as its first executive director. From 1922 to 1947, Haynes was in charge of the Commission on Race Relations for the Federal Council of Churches, a national organization of different Christian denominations formed to encourage ecumenical discussion and cooperation. He wrote extensively about issues of race and religion and established local discussion groups to bring whites and blacks together to study, to talk, and to act to solve racial problems within their own communities.

Gordon Blaine Hancock, a black Baptist minister and college professor from Richmond, Virginia, organized the Conference on Race Relations, an important meeting of Southern black leaders held in Durham, North Carolina, in 1942. This all-black meeting produced a statement called the Durham Manifesto, which challenged white

Southern leaders to cooperate with blacks to improve race relations. As a result, the Southern Regional Council, one of the few interracial organizations in the pre–civil rights South, was founded in 1943 at Atlanta University. Given the situation of discrimination and the climate of racism, these were significant achievements for the time.

Black ministers and congregations also established networks of cooperation across denominational lines. During the 1930s, for example, ministers in Harlem organized boycotts against stores and agencies that refused to hire black employees, advising their congregations from the pulpit, "Don't buy where you can't work." In 1933, a group of black clergymen organized the National Fraternal Council of Negro Churches to promote cooperation among different denominations for both social and religious causes. During the 1940s and 1950s the Fraternal Council protested racial discrimination and lobbied Congress to pass civil rights legislation.

One of the earliest and most influential proponents of interracial and interfaith community was the black minister, university chaplain, and author Howard Thurman. Born in 1900 in Daytona, Florida, Thurman was raised in the Baptist church. As a child, he had a profound religious experience in which he felt himself to be at one with all of the natural world. He received support for his spiritual sensitivity from his mother and his grandmother, who was a former slave. Thurman studied at Morehouse College and Rochester Theological Seminary, excelling in his schoolwork. After seminary he accepted an offer to serve as pastor of a Baptist church in Oberlin, Ohio. From there he moved on to become chaplain at Howard University in Washington, D.C., and Dean of the Chapel at Boston University.

In 1935 the YMCA sent a delegation of African Americans to India, including Thurman and his wife, Sue Bailey Thurman. After lecturing in Calcutta, Thurman was brought up short by a conversation with an Indian lawyer who demanded to know how

Howard Thurman was famous for his ability to reach listerners, both black and white, through his sermons.

Thurman, whose people had been enslaved and oppressed by Christians, could still believe in Christianity. Thurman responded that "the religion of Jesus in its true genius" supported "freedom, liberty, and justice for all people, black, white, red, yellow, saint, sinner, rich, or poor." He developed this theme of the significance of Jesus for the poor and oppressed more fully in one of his many books, *Jesus and the Disinherited* (1949).

In India, the Thurmans also met with Mahatma Gandhi, the spiritual leader, agitator for India's independence from British control, and advocate of nonviolent resistance to social evil. The Thurmans spoke with him about the situation of black Americans in comparison with the outcastes of India. At the end of their conversation, Gandhi asked them to sing for him "Were You There When They Crucified My Lord," which he said "gets to the root of the experience of the entire human race under the spread of the healing wings of suffering." Thurman shared his own interpretation of the wisdom of the spirituals in the books *Deep River* (1945) and *The Negro Spiritual Speaks of Life and Death* (1947), which was first delivered as a lecture at Harvard Divinity School. He was deeply convinced that the legacy of slave religion was of lasting importance: "By some amazing but vastly creative spiritual insight, the slave undertook the redemption of a religion that the master had profaned in his midst." In 1944, Thurman became pastor of the Church for the Fellowship of All Peoples in San Francisco, California, one of the first, if not *the* first, interfaith and interracial churches in the country.

A steady stream of sermons, meditations, and essays, published over the next three decades, circulated Thurman's thoughts on spiritual growth, mysticism, community, and race to a large audience across the country and around the world. Noted as one of the great preachers of his day, he influenced people of many different races and religions by the power of his personal presence and the spiritual authority of his message.

In 1954 the U.S. Supreme Court declared in the case of *Brown v. Board of Education* that racially separate schools were inherently unequal, thus striking down the principle of separate but equal that the Court had established in the *Plessy v. Ferguson* decision of 1896. The *Brown* decision ordered the end of separate schools "with all deliberate speed," but

On September 15, 1963 a powerful bomb exploded in the 16th Street Baptist Church of Birmingham, killing four black girls. The tragedy shocked the nation and created support for federal legislation to protect the civil rights of black Americans.

Southern schools, not to mention lunch counters, restaurants, train and bus stations, washrooms, hotels, drinking fountains, movie theaters, courthouses, and churches, remained segregated for years to come.

On December 1, 1955, a black seamstress named Rosa Parks boarded a bus in Montgomery, Alabama. Buses in Montgomery had always been segregated. Blacks sat in back; whites sat up front. If the bus was full, blacks were required to give up their seats to whites and ride standing in the aisle. Mrs. Parks found a seat in the front of the section reserved for "Colored" and sat down. As the bus grew crowded with people heading home from work, no seats were available for new passengers boarding the bus, so the driver ordered Mrs. Parks and three other black passengers to get up and give their seats to whites. The others obeyed, but Rosa Parks stayed seated until a policeman came and placed her under arrest.

News of her arrest spread quickly in the black community. That evening, several black women, some of them active in the local Women's

Political Council, decided that they should respond by refusing to ride the buses. They suggested the idea to E.D. Nixon, director of the local NAACP in Montgomery, and he began phoning black ministers and other community leaders to mobilize a boycott. For almost a year blacks in Montgomery stopped riding the buses, even though many of them depended on the bus for transportation to work. Instead, they walked or arranged car pools to take them where they needed to go. On November 13, 1956, they won: the U.S. Supreme Court upheld a lower court decision that declared Alabama laws requiring segregation on buses unconstitutional. These two events, the *Brown* decision of the Supreme Court in 1954 and the successful Montgomery bus boycott in 1955–56, ushered in a new period in the struggle of African Americans for racial justice. They inspired a new attitude of hope and activism among African Americans intent on gaining equal rights.

The Montgomery bus boycott also brought to national attention the 26-year-old pastor of the city's Dexter Avenue Baptist Church, Martin Luther King, Jr. King, who had recently moved to Montgomery, had neither suggested nor started the boycott, but he was chosen to be its spokesman anyway. Born in 1929 in Atlanta to Alberta Williams and the Reverend Martin L. King, Sr., King was shaped from childhood by the black church.

He quickly made his reputation as an excellent preacher. Throughout the civil rights movement, King drew upon the black church tradition to inspire the movement's participants, both black and white. He, and others, perceived his leadership as religious and his authority as moral. His style of speaking, his choice of words and images, and the rhythm of his speeches and sermons all echoed his church background and brought to mind the moral authority of the black religious tradition. In his very first address as the president of the Montgomery Improvement Association, King spoke to a packed audience in the Mount Zion AME Zion Church at the start of the bus boycott on December 5, 1955. He defined the black freedom struggle as a moral and religious cause:

> [W]e are not wrong in what we are doing. If we are wrong, then the Supreme Court of this nation is wrong. If we are wrong, the Constitution of the United

Martin Luther King, Jr., and Coretta Scott King attend a celebration in their honor at Dexter Avenue Baptist Church in Montgomery, Alabama. As pastor of this church, King became the spokesman for the Montgomery bus boycott and attracted national fame.

States is wrong. If we are wrong, God Almighty is wrong. If we are wrong, Jesus of Nazareth was merely a utopian dreamer and never came down to earth. If we are wrong, justice is a lie. And we are determined here in Montgomery to work and fight until justice runs down like water, and righteousness like a mighty stream.

King's defense of the civil rights movement on moral and religious principles, and his assertion that it was the most important religious cause of the day, was opposed by many citizens who saw civil rights as only a political fight between Southern white conservatives and black radical agitators. Christian ethics, they argued, were a matter of personal morality, not social action. According to King, the struggle for civil rights presented the nation with a historic opportunity to solve its greatest moral failure—racial prejudice and discrimination. In linking political action and religion, he was following the example of his elders. In 1935 his father, Martin Luther King, Sr., led several thousand black demonstrators in support of black citizens' right to vote. And a decade earlier, his grandfather, the Reverend Adam Daniel Williams, organized demonstrations to demand funding for black high school education.

During his undergraduate years at Morehouse College in Atlanta, King began to think systematically about race in the United States and its relationship to Christianity. He read Henry David Thoreau's "Essay on Civil Disobedience" and absorbed the idea that it is every individual's moral duty to refuse to cooperate with an evil system. Later he studied at Crozier Seminary in Pennsylvania and was influenced by the thinking of Christian theologians who emphasized the application of Christian ethics to the problems of society. He also heard a lecture by Mordecai Johnson, the president of Howard University, on the life and philosophy of Mahatma Gandhi. Gandhi's nonviolent campaign to gain India's independence from Great Britain had been reported in the black press and had attracted widespread interest and admiration among black Americans of all walks of life. Hearing about Gandhi inspired King to study the Indian leader's ideas about the use of nonviolent resistance. At Boston University's School of Theology, King studied the major Western philosophers and learned about personalism, a mode of thought that stressed the primary value of each human being.

Though strongly attracted to the academic life, King decided that he could best serve the cause of social justice by returning to ministerial work in the South. Therefore, he accepted an offer to serve as pastor of the Dexter Avenue Baptist Church in Montgomery in 1954. In 1957 King joined with other black ministers (who were mostly Baptists) in forming the Southern Christian Leadership Conference (SCLC).

King's colleagues and assistants in the SCLC included Ralph Abernathy, his friend and fellow pastor from Montgomery; Andrew Young, a Congregationalist minister from New Orleans who would later become mayor of Atlanta, Georgia; James Lawson, ordained in the United Methodist Church; Wyatt T. Walker, a Baptist clergyman; Jesse Jackson, another Baptist minister (who would later run for President several times); and Ella Baker, one of the leaders of the civil rights movement. Baker helped organize the SCLC, serving as its first executive secretary, and she also helped to form the Student Non-Violent Coordinating

Committee (SNCC), a group of young activists who led protests and attempted to register black voters across the South. Following on the success of the Montgomery bus boycott, SCLC leaders hoped to organize and coordinate similar antisegregation efforts in other communities. As the president of the SCLC, King traveled and spoke extensively, preaching a philosophy of nonviolent protest.

It was necessary for black people to protest against segregation, King argued, to avoid cooperating with an evil system. If one passively accepted injustice, one enabled it to continue. Therefore demonstrations, marches, rallies, and boycotts were necessary, even if they disturbed the peace, because they broke down the false social order that masked the true disorder of injustice lying beneath the surface. Demonstrations created so much civic tension that white authorities in city after city had to respond; they could no longer ignore the issue of race.

To those who argued that the time was not right for protest, King replied, "We have waited for more than 340 years for our constitutional and God-given rights . . . we are tired—tired of being segregated and humiliated; tired of being kicked about by the brutal feet of oppression." Now was the time to protest. To those who objected that demonstrations encouraged lawlessness, Keng answered that sometimes obeying a higher law required breaking an unjust law and enduring the punishment. Besides, the reaction of white mobs to black protest revealed who was truly lawless. When white police attacked unarmed black demonstrators with clubs, cattle prods, fire hoses, and police dogs, the lawlessness of racism stood revealed, captured on film for the nation, indeed the entire world, to see. And many were shocked to see that such things could happen in the United States.

King argued that blacks had to use nonviolent methods to achieve their goals, not only because violence had no chance of success, but because nonviolence was the morally superior way to act. Nonviolence was not simply a political tactic, it was a way of life, the perfect method for translating Christian love into social action. King explained that nonviolence was a form of active, not passive, resistance. Nonviolence was based upon the firm conviction that suffering was redemptive because it

Bombs in Birmingham

On September 15, 1963, a bomb shattered the front of the 16th Street Baptist Church in Birmingham, Alabama. Four children died in the blast: Denise McNair, 11, Addie Mae Collins, 14, Carole Robertson, 14, and Cynthia Wesley, 14. The Reverend Martin Luther King, Jr., preached the following funeral sermon.

These children—unoffending, innocent and beautiful—were the victims of one of the most vicious, heinous crimes ever perpetrated agianst humanity. . . . They are the martyred heroines of a holy crusade for freedom and human dignity. So they have something to say to us in their death. They have something to say to every minister of the gospel who has remained silent behind the safe security of stained-glass windows. They have something to say to every politician who has fed his constituents the stale bread of hatred and the spoiled meat of racism. . . . They have something to say to each of us, black and white alike, that we must substitute courage for caution. . . . Their death says to us that we must work passionately and unrelentingly to make the American dream a reality. So they did not die in vain.

God still has a way of wringing good out of evil. History has proven over and over again that unmerited suffering is redemptive. The innocent blood of these little girls may well serve as the redemptive force that will bring new light to this dark city. . . . So in spite of the darkness of this hour we must not despair. We must not become bitter; nor must we harbor the desire to retaliate with violence. We must not lose faith in our white brothers. Somehow we must believe that the most misguided among them can learn to respect the dignity and worth of all human personality.

could transform both the sufferer and the oppressor; it tried to convert, not to defeat, the opponent; and it was based on the confidence that justice would, in the end, win out over injustice. By accepting the violence of the racist, without the desire for revenge and even without hatred or bitterness, the demonstrators believed they could change the racist's heart.

For King, and those who followed his leadership, the goal of the civil rights movement was "to save the soul of the nation." The civil rights movement became a religious crusade. The demonstrations themselves took on the feel of church services. They began with rallies usually held in black churches and followed a pattern of song, prayer, Bible reading, discussion of goals, and speeches that often resembled sermons. Traditional songs, such as "Keep Your Eyes on the Prize," stirred up memories of previous generations and their struggles against slavery and oppression. New songs, such as "We Shall Overcome," created a sense of group solidarity and communal strength. From the churches, the demonstrators moved out into the public streets to bear witness to the cause of freedom and equality. Some of them, white as well as black, gave their lives. Although King attracted widespread support among white and black Protestants, Catholics, Jews, and people of no particular religion, he also received a great deal of criticism, even within the black church. Some disagreed with his philosophy of social activism because they believed that society could only be changed by converting individuals to obey God's commandments, not by mass political agitation. Others, like Joseph H. Jackson, the president of the largest black Baptist denomination, believed that legal solutions to discrimination already existed and would work if given time, without irresponsible demonstrators stirring up counterproductive anger and violence. The strongest criticism of King's theory and practice of nonviolent resistance came from the chief spokesman for the Nation of Islam, Malcolm X. Malcolm preached that African Americans, like any other people, had a right to gain their freedom "by any means necessary," including violence. He rejected the SCLC's tactics and argued that separatism and self-determination were necessary for blacks to achieve full equality.

Malcolm X was born Malcolm Little in 1925 in Omaha, Nebraska. His father, the Reverend Earl Little, a Baptist preacher and an active promoter of the ideals of Marcus Garvey, died in a mysterious accident when Malcolm was six years old, causing him to suspect that his father had been murdered by white racists. Tragedy struck again several years later when his mother suffered an emotional breakdown and was placed in a mental institution. Malcolm's family was broken up, and he and his eight siblings were separated in different foster homes. Shifted from home to home, he grew up with no refuge or protection from the hostility of white society. For example, a white teacher at school mocked his desire to make something of himself by telling him that his ambition to become a lawyer was not a realistic goal for blacks.

Disillusioned by hopelessness, Malcolm dropped out of school in the eighth grade. He drifted into criminal activity as a teenager, hanging out with gamblers and drug dealers in Boston and Harlem. Eventually he was arrested for burglary and sentenced to prison. There another inmate convinced him that he needed to learn to think and to speak clearly in order to improve himself. He began a rigorous program of self-education to improve his vocabulary and his knowledge through reading. Around the same time, he learned from one of his brothers about the teachings of Elijah Muhammad and the Nation of Islam.

As he later recalled in the *Autobiography of Malcolm X,* which he wrote with Alex Haley, the message of the black Muslims hit him with the force of a revelation and turned his life completely around. The moral discipline of the Nation—its stress on regular prayer, fasting, almsgiving, and obedience of the will of Allah, and its rejection of alcohol, tobacco, and drugs—gave stability to his daily life and boosted his self-esteem. The Nation's account of human origins explained to his satisfaction the source of the white racism that had continually limited the possibilities of his life.

After his release from prison, Malcolm became a minister for the Nation, first in Boston and then in Harlem, rising rapidly to positions of greater leadership thanks to his exceptional speaking ability, charismatic personality, energy, and organizational skill. He founded a newspaper called *Muhammad Speaks* to spread the doctrines of Messenger Elijah

Muhammad and to interpret national and world events from the black Muslim perspective. Finally, he was appointed national representative, second to Elijah Muhammad himself. A forceful debater, Malcolm appeared on television, radio talk shows, college campuses, and press interviews around the country, arguing for black separatism and attacking the idea of integration. Blacks, he said, needed to recover their true identity as Muslims and to begin to act for themselves instead of wasting their efforts trying to convert the white devils. As proof of the Nation's teachings, he pointed to the Black Muslims' success at reforming ex-convicts, drug addicts, and alcoholics. In his scathing criticism of the hypocrisy about race showed by whites in the United States, he eloquently expressed the anger that many blacks felt about their unequal treatment in a supposedly free and equal society.

Malcolm X, an electrifying orator, speaks at a rally commemorating Marcus Garvey Day in Harlem. Malcolm's father and mother had supported Garvey's ideals.

After President John F. Kennedy's assassination in 1963, Malcolm made comments to the press that seemed critical of the dead president. Elijah Muhammad disapproved of these remarks and responded by suspending him. Malcolm, for his part, had already become disillusioned with Elijah Muhammad over reports about the Messenger's moral life. In 1964, he left the Nation of Islam and organized his own Muslim Mosque, Inc., in New York City. A few weeks later Malcolm went on the hajj, the pilgrimage to Mecca that is prescribed as a religious duty for all Muslims. There he was amazed to experience truly interracial fellowship with Muslims of all colors and races from around the world. Deeply moved, Malcolm accepted orthodox Islam and became a Sunni Muslim, taking the name el-Hajj Malik el-Shabazz.

Upon his return he began speaking out against the Nation of Islam and its Messenger. A tour of African states led him to think of the problems of blacks in the United States as part of the international struggle of Third World peoples for human rights. In 1965, he founded the

Organization for Afro-American Unity to link the cause of black Americans with the cause of oppressed people in Africa and elsewhere. Shortly thereafter he was assassinated as he delivered a speech at the Audubon Ballroom in Harlem.

His early death and the subsequent publication of the *Autobiography of Malcolm X* extended Malcolm's influence and allowed him and his ideas to become more widely appreciated than they were during his lifetime. His uncompromising criticism of racism, as well as his emphasis on blacks standing up for their rights and protecting themselves, appealed to many as a welcome example of black courage, discipline, and pride. And his willingness to express black anger offered a counterbalance to the emotional restraint required by the practice of nonviolence.

Optimism about the nonviolent crusade for civil rights peaked from 1963 to 1965. During these years, the March on Washington brought more than 200,000 white and black citizens to the nation's capital to demand the passage of civil rights legislation by Congress. The march climaxed with King's famous "I Have a Dream" speech, which he delivered on the steps of the Lincoln Memorial on August 28, 1963. In eloquent words that moved thousands and that would be repeated time and time again after his death, King spoke of his dream "that one day this nation will rise up and live out the true meaning of its creed—we hold these truths to be self-evident that all men are created equal." Demonstrations in Selma, Alabama, in March 1965 attracted widespread interracial and interfaith support for the cause, and the passage of a major civil rights bill by Congress in 1964 seemed to indicate that discrimination was in full retreat. At that time King's dream was still "deeply rooted in the American dream," as he claimed at the March on Washington. But rioting in black neighborhoods in Detroit, the Watts section of Los Angeles, and other metropolitan areas around the nation, the escalation of the Vietnam War, and the failure of demonstrations to effect change in northern cities like Chicago threatened the dream that seemed so possible in 1963.

Despite opposition from many of his advisors, King began to speak out against the Vietnam War in 1967. He viewed the war as morally evil, a diversion of money and energy from the war on poverty and racism that needed to be waged at home. In his most famous antiwar speech, delivered at Riverside Church in New York City, he attacked "the deadly Western arrogance that has poisoned the international atmosphere for so long." He accused the nation of being on the wrong side of the revolutions against poverty and injustice that were taking place all over the world. And he argued that the United States had to shift from being a "thing-ordered society to a person-oriented society" if the evils of racism, materialism, and militarism were ever going to be conquered.

Increasingly concerned about the relationship between racism and the unfair distribution of wealth in the economy, King was planning to organize a "Poor People's Campaign, which would bring together poor people of all races to fight their common enemy, economic oppression." While he was doing this, King accepted an invitation to join demonstrations to support striking sanitation workers in Memphis, Tennessee. He was assassinated in Memphis on April 4, 1968. The night before he was killed, he gave a speech that drew upon the biblical images of the old slave spirituals to instill hope and at the same time seemed to anticipate his own death:

> We've got some difficult days ahead. But it really doesn't matter with me now. Because I've been to the mountaintop. Like anybody I would like to live a long life. Longevity has its place. But I'm not concerned about that now. I just want to do God's will. And He's allowed me to go up to the mountain. And I've *seen* the Promised Land. And I may not get there with you. But I want you to know tonight that we as a people will get to the Promised Land.

During the last years of King's life, disappointment with the slow pace of change and disagreement over the tactic of nonviolence had led some black activists to formulate a demand for "black power" in 1966. Black power quickly became a rallying cry for those who thought King's approach was no longer effective. King's assassination seemed to confirm that the period of nonviolent protest had passed and led to massive

VOL. V, No. 1: 1977

THE MAGAZINE OF BLACK LITURGY PUBLISHED BY THE NATIONAL OFFICE FOR BLACK CATHOLICS

Freeing the Spirit

Roman Catholic sisters on the cover of *Freeing the Spirit* prepare to celebrate Mass. During the 1970s black Catholics added African-style rituals to worship services to recognize and celebrate their African-American cultural heritage.

rioting in cities around the country. Some activists accused religious institutions of being otherworldly, conservative, and an obstacle to black liberation. The ideal of integration was replaced by calls for liberation, self-determination, and community control. Black pride and the celebration of black culture represented a new mood of independence among African Americans. Separatism was on the rise, even in church circles.

In 1967, black delegates to a National Council of Churches conference insisted on splitting the meeting into two sections, one black and one white. Black Christians in predominantly white churches established ongoing separate offices or caucuses to deal with issues of black identity and black power. For example, between 1968 and 1970, black Catholics organized the Black Catholic Clergy Caucus, the National Black Sisters Conference, the Black Catholic Lay Caucus, and finally the National Office of Black Catholics. In this setting of separatism, black pride, and the celebration of black people's African heritage, black Christians in predominantly white churches began to raise questions about the relationship between their religious and their racial identities.

One answer was provided by black theology, an attempt by black Christian scholars to examine systematically the distinctive character of African-American religious experience. The most prominent black theologian was James H. Cone, a professor at Union Theological Seminary in New York, whose first book, *Black Theology and Black Power,* appeared in 1969. As the title suggests, Cone's book was partly a response to the challenge presented to black Christians by the black power movement. What did Christianity have to do with the liberation of black people? Cone's answer, further developed in succeeding books, was that God identifies himself in human history with the struggle of black people and has promised the ultimate liberation of the oppressed through the life, death, and resurrection of Jesus. Cone's theology stressed the theme of liberation; other black theologians emphasized reconciliation between the races. Cone, and black theology generally, was criticized for using white academic vocabulary to describe the religious experience of black people. African American theologians soon entered into discussions with liberation theologians in Latin America and black theologians in Africa.

King's assassination marked the end of an identifiable movement for racial equality on the national level. No black leader of national stature has managed to take his place, though some have tried. The absence of a national movement has distracted observers from considering the activity of black churches on the local level in matters of community organization, housing, education, economic development, and employment. In numerous black communities, black churches sponsored housing improvements, neighborhood development programs, health-care clinics, day-care centers, and activities for senior citizens. Moreover, leaders like King or Malcolm X are important, but people like them do not come along often. Their lives should not overshadow the heroism of the ordinary people who marched, participated in sit-in demonstrations and boycotts, and risked their lives because they wanted freedom for themselves and for their children. For them black freedom was a religious cause that challenged them to act and stirred the conscience of the whole nation. Throughout the civil rights phase of the black freedom struggle, black churches served as the institutional backbone of the movement. But beyond their organizational role, it was their members who provided the movement with its soul.

Just as in the 19th-century antislavery movement, it seemed as if this was a period of historic importance for the meaning of the U.S. experiment in democracy. Just as in the 19th century, the test case for the success or failure of the experiment was the situation of African Americans. The civil rights movement of the 1950s and 1960s forced many Americans to ask themselves, as the freedom song simply put it, "Which Side Are You On?"

Chapter 7

Black Faith: Continuity Within Change

During the last half of the 20th century, large-scale economic, political, social, and cultural changes have swept the nation and profoundly affected the religious lives and institutions of African Americans. Migration, urbanization, and the civil rights movement fundamentally altered the conditions of life for African Americans. In this context, the church has served both as a source of stability and as a vehicle of change. By preserving the traditions of African-American culture, black churches helped black communities and individuals experience continuity with the past. By calling up familiar religious stories, such as Exodus, or images, such as the Promised Land, to explain new circumstances, black pastors helped their people to adjust to rapid change. The churches not only reacted to social and political change; they also participated in making it happen.

In 1975 Elijah Muhammad died, and his son Wallace Deen Muhammad succeeded to the leadership of the Nation of Islam. Rapidly, he began to move the members of the Nation toward embracing orthodox Islam by explaining that the teachings of Wallace D. Fard and his father should be understood symbolically, not literally. Abandoning the separatism of his father, he opened the Nation of Islam to white membership and encouraged his followers to participate in political elections as citizens of the United States. The organization symbolized

Elijah Muhammad, leader of the Nation of Islam for most of its history, sits next to his son and successor Wallace (Warithuddin) Muhammad beneath a painting of W.D. Fard, the founder of the Nation.

its radical changes in philosophy by changing its name, first to the World Community of Islam in the West, and later to the American Muslim Mission. The ministers were renamed "imams," a word used by Sunni Muslims, one of the two main branches of Islam in the world, to refer to their leaders; and Wallace Muhammad (who had been named for Wallace D. Fard) became Warithuddin Muhammad. In 1987 Warithuddin Muhammad disbanded the entire organization and urged its members to simply join orthodox local mosques. These changes were rejected by some black Muslims, who, under the leadership of Minister Louis Farrakhan, returned to the original teachings and ideals of Elijah Muhammad and readopted the group's old name, the Nation of Islam.

Growing numbers of black Americans converted to worldwide Islam independently of the Nation or other racially specific forms of Islam. Islam proved to be an attractive religious alternative to black converts, especially black men. One estimate made in 1989 placed the number of African-American Muslims at 1 million, out of a total of 6 million Muslims in the United States. The conversion of prominent black athletes such as Muhammad Ali (who changed his name from Cassius Clay) and Kareem Abdul-Jabbar (formerly Lew Alcindor), as well as the active ministry of Muslims to the black population in prisons, contributed to the visibility of Islam among younger black men. Islam appealed also to black women and black families. Dr. Betty Shabazz, the widow of Malcolm X, served as a model of achievement by a black female Muslim. When she died in 1997, her funeral took place at the Sunni mosque on 96th Street in New York City, illustrating the acceptance by African Americans of worldwide Islam.

During the last half of the century, the number of black Catholics increased dramatically as a result of conversions. Between 1940 and 1975, the black Catholic population grew from 296,988 to 916,854—an increase of 208 percent. Black Catholics grew from 2.3 percent to 4 percent of the black population as a whole. Since 1975 the rate of conversions has slowed, but the immigration of black Catholics from the Caribbean and Latin America has increased the total black Catholic population to more than 2 million.

In the 1970s and 1980s, the National Office of Black Catholics, the Institute for Black Catholic Studies at Xavier University, and local communities of black Catholics sought to define the meaning of Catholicism for themselves by developing new African-American forms of worship, theology, and ministry, and by reclaiming black Catholic history. In some predominantly black parishes, African music, drumming, and dance, as well as black Protestant gospel music, were added to the Catholic Mass in an attempt to create a worship service more attuned to traditional forms of black cultural expression. In 1984, the 10 black Catholic bishops of the United States issued a pastoral letter, "What We Have Seen and Heard," calling for black Catholics to tell the lessons of their history for the benefit of the entire Church. And in 1987 the first African-American Catholic Congress in 90 years met in New Orleans, consciously recalling the heritage of the black Catholic congresses of the late 19th century.

Migration of blacks out of the South slowed by the 1950s and reversed in the 1960s, as a larger proportion of black people moved South than left. However, another large-scale movement of people, this time from outside the country, made a new and surprising contribution to the variety of African-American religions. Immigrants from Cuba and Haiti have introduced the traditional spirits of Africa to the United States. The religions of Santería and Vodou, which originated during slavery in Cuba and Haiti and were practiced by slaves in European colonies in Africa as well, spread in black and Hispanic communities across the country. Here, as in Cuba and Haiti, the members celebrated the feasts of the spirits in rituals of drumming, singing, and dancing that derived ultimately from West and Central Africa. These rituals expressed the belief that the spirits ruled over all aspects of life. By offering them praise and sacrifice, people won their favor and gained their powerful assistance in times of illness or misfortune. In ceremonies of spirit trance, believers made contact between divinity and humanity possible by embodying the spirits for the community. Whenever something went wrong, priests determined the cause and prescribed the proper offerings and prayers to set things right. In these ways, Santería and Vodou maintained a view of life as personal and relational in the midst of the impersonality of modern-day society in the United States.

The number of North American blacks who converted to these African-derived religions was growing. Beginning in the 1960s, new interest in their African heritage prompted some African Americans to adopt African names, styles of dress, and religious traditions. Books and classes on African religious traditions enabled black Americans to become better informed about African spirituality and practice. Yoruba and Yoruba-derived religious communities in Nigeria, Cuba, Brazil, and the United States established formal links with one another by instituting annual "Orisa Tradition" conferences (*orisa* being the Yoruba word for divinity). In 1986, the third conference was held in New York City. The ancient religions of Africa proved to fit very well into the modern world.

Black theology was developed by a whole new generation of black female theologians. Critical of black male theologians for failing to take account of their experience, these women took the name "womanist" to distinguish themselves from white feminists, who neglected the issue of race. Womanist theology took as its starting point the experience of black women, including their experiences of the triple evils of racism, sexism, and poverty (because black women made up a relatively high proportion of the poor). Looking to 19th-century pioneers such as Sojourner Truth and Jarena Lee, and to 20th-century literary figures such as Zora Neale Hurston and Alice Walker, for ideas and inspiration, womanist theologians suggested new ways of interpreting ethics, the Bible, and the significance of Jesus, from the perspective of black women. Leading womanist theologians of the time included Katie Cannon, Delores Williams, and Jacquelyn Grant.

In her book *Black Womanist Ethics* (1988), Katie Cannon used the fiction of Zora Neale Hurston to examine the folktales and stories that black people, and especially black women, have used to express moral lessons and popular wisdom. In the stories of black women's lives, she found examples of their ability to rise above the limits of racism, sexism, and poverty in order to give value and significance to themselves, their families, and their communities.

Delores Williams, in *Sisters in the Wilderness* (1993), reflected on the biblical story of the slave Hagar, who was driven into the desert, along with her child Ishmael, by Abraham's jealous wife, Sarah. There, exhausted and desperate, she was saved by God, who promised that her son Ishmael would be the father of a great nation. This story, Williams argued, offered an alternative to mainstream biblical interpretation that has concentrated on Sarah and her son Isaac. The experience of Hagar represented a model of faith, hope, and strength for black women, who, like her, were enslaved and "driven into the wilderness" of despair by the oppression of white society.

Jacquelyn Grant, writing in *White Woman's Christ, Black Woman's Jesus* (1989), depicted Jesus as the "divine co-sufferer, who empowers [black people] in situations of oppression." If Christ identified himself with the poor and the oppressed, then today he identifies in particular with black women, triply oppressed by racism, sexism, and poverty. Echoing the views of Jarena Lee, Grant argued that if Christ died for all humanity, then the views and experiences of black women should not be left out of the theology of the Church, nor should black women be denied leadership roles in Christian congregations.

The issue of the ordination of black women as pastors continued to stir controversy. Though the African Methodist Episcopal Zion Church had ordained Julia Foote in 1894, the African Methodist Episcopal Church did not ordain a woman until 1948, and the Christian Methodist Episcopal Church did not follow until 1954. Women in the three main

Katie Cannon, a professor at Temple University, is one of several scholars whose work analyzes the religious experience of black American women.

black Baptist denominations continued to face difficulty in seeking ordination. No official national policy prohibited it, but most of the independent Baptist congregations refused to allow women to be ordained, although in recent years a small number of black ministers have sponsored women candidates for ordination. Once ordained, black Baptist women have found it difficult to convince congregations to call them pastors. The Church of God in Christ, the largest black Pentecostal denomination, allowed women to preach as missionaries or evangelists, but officially opposed the ordination of women as pastors, although in a few cases widows were allowed to continue temporarily the pastoral duties of their husbands. Black women did receive ordination in predominantly white denominations that permitted the ordination of women, such as the Unitarian-Universalists, the United Church of Christ, and the Episcopalians, who elected a black woman, Barbara C. Harris, as a bishop in 1988.

Celebrations of Malcolm X and Martin Luther King, Jr., spread awareness of their lives and their causes to more people, with King's birthday observed as a holiday in most states and Malcolm's legacy of black pride and self-respect claimed by a new generation of black youth. On the national political scene, the Reverend Jesse Jackson attempted to revive the spirit of the civil rights movement in his 1984 and 1988 campaigns to be nominated as the Democratic party's Presidential candidate. Black churches played an important role in the local organization of his campaigns, sponsoring rallies, enlisting volunteers, registering people to vote, and transporting voters to the polling booths. Following the precedent of Adam Clayton Powell, Jr., a pastor of Abyssinian Baptist Church in Harlem who served in the House of Representatives during the 1950s and 1960s, individual ministers used the power base of large urban congregations to get elected to Congress. For example, the Reverend Floyd Flake, of Allen AME Church in Queens, served several terms as a congressman from New York until he retired in 1998 to return to full-time pastoral activity. And ministers in big cities such as Chicago, New York, and Atlanta often wielded considerable power in local urban politics.

On the local level, black churches have acted to solve problems of community organization, education, economic development, and employment, as they often have in the past. For instance, in 1964, the Reverend Leon Sullivan, pastor of Zion Baptist Church in Philadelphia, established the Opportunities Industrialization Center (OIC), a highly successful and widely imitated model of church-sponsored economic development. The OIC trained unemployed black and white workers for skilled positions in industry and helped them find jobs to match their new skills. By the end of the decade, similar OIC programs had been set up in various cities across the country.

Black churches have also tried to improve the substandard housing of inner-city black communities. In one noteworthy example, Abyssinian Baptist built housing for the elderly and renovated rundown apartments for the homeless in Harlem under the leadership of the Reverend Samuel Proctor, who succeeded Adam Clayton Powell, Jr., as pastor of the church from 1972 to 1989. Since then Abyssinian Baptist has continued to build and renovate housing in rundown Harlem neighborhoods through the Abyssinian Development Corporation. Samuel Proctor's successor, the Reverend Calvin Butts, has spoken out regularly on issues of concern to the black community, specifically criticizing cigarette and liquor advertisers for targeting black consumers.

In 1945 Father Shelton Hale Bishop, the rector of St. Philip's Episcopal Church in Harlem, provided space for the Lafargue Clinic, the first mental health facility for African Americans. The clinic provided psychiatric care to Harlem residents until 1960. Dr. Moran Weston, who succeeded Father Bishop at St. Philip's, led in the development of Bishop House and Weston House as residences for homeless and mentally ill men and women. Dr. Weston had already built St. Philip's Senior House for the elderly, the Community Service Council of Greater Harlem, and the Greater Harlem Nursing Home to serve the needs of the surrounding community.

Bridge Street African Wesleyan Methodist Episcopal Church in Brooklyn, led by the Reverend Fred Lucas since 1982, followed in the footsteps of the black churches of the 1930s by developing an extensive outreach program. Bridge Street Church stayed open from 9 A.M. to 10 P.M. most days of the week to accommodate the 60 clubs and auxiliaries that met there regularly. Church-sponsored programs included distributing food to the poor, counseling alcoholics and drug addicts, helping the unemployed find work, and teaching classes for adults seeking high school equivalency diplomas. Similarly, St. Paul Community Baptist Church in East New York, led by the Reverend Johnny Youngblood since 1974, built an elementary school and a high school, and joined with other churches in the Nehemiah Project, whose purpose was to construct low-income housing in Brownsville and East New York.

All across the country, black churches have needed to establish more economic and social programs because of cutbacks in state and federal programs that began in the early 1980s. Because of cuts in tax money for these programs, less public assistance became available for the homeless, the poor, the elderly, children, and the mentally ill. Therefore, private organizations—which in the black community meant primarily the churches—have had to step in to attempt to help some of the neediest citizens in the United States.

For most of the past 50 years, scholars have asserted that modern secular attitudes were lessening the power of the black church in the black community. In the 1980s and 1990s, social analysts have blamed the loss of religious values among inner-city blacks as a major cause of the crises of teenage pregnancies, illegitimate births, fatherless households, drug abuse, and "black on black" crime. Yet the same commentators looked to the black church as the primary community agency to deal with these difficult problems of poverty and unemployment. Many black churches have attempted to raise public awareness of these conditions and have urged their members to take personal responsibility for improving their communities. At the same time, though, they recognized that the devastation of the inner cities was a long-term social and economic problem that required national solutions, especially more government assistance.

In 1996, the largest gathering of black men in the nation's history gathered on the Mall in Washington, D.C., for a day of atonement and reconciliation. Atonement and reconciliation are religious concepts, and the event offered the black men who attended a kind of public ritual that would allow them to repent for failing to care adequately for their

Louis Farrakhan gives an impassioned speech at the Million Man March on the Mall in Washington, D.C. Farrakhan organized and led the day of atonement and reconciliation.

families and their communities and to dedicate themselves to doing better. The Million Man March, as it was called, drew hundreds of thousands of participants in spite of controversy over its organizer, Nation of Islam leader Minister Louis Farrakhan, as well as the opinion of some people that black men, who had suffered generations of social and economic discrimination, had no reason to apologize.

A sociological study by C. Eric Lincoln and Lawrence Mamiya, published in 1990, examined the seven largest black religious bodies and found that while on the whole black churches remained numerically strong and influential institutions, they faced major challenges from a growing division in the black community between middle-class blacks and the poor unemployed. The study also noted that the churches had lost their influence over urban lower-class youth (especially young men), and observed the growing attraction of Islam.

Statistics show that black churches have indeed remained strong over the last 50 years. In 1936 (the last year the government gathered such figures) the U.S. Census for Religious Bodies estimated that there were 5.7 million church members in a black population of 12.8 million. According to the 1986 edition of the *Yearbook of American and Canadian Churches*, black Baptists numbered more than 9 million, black Methodists roughly 4 million, and the black Holiness-Pentecostal family probably exceeded 4 million members. While these figures, based on church reports, were probably overstated, a large percentage of the black population of the United States are church members. Yet the effectiveness of social programs and the size of membership rolls are not the only, nor necessarily the most revealing, ways of measuring the black church's significance. The centrality of the church in the African American's search for identity and meaning has demonstrated its ongoing adaptability and stability during a period of rapid and unsettling change.

Institutional church life has played a key role in the social and cultural life of black communities for more than two centuries. And religion has had a profound influence in the individual lives of black people. Although there have always been people who choose not to believe or practice any religion, the overwhelming majority of African Americans have identified with some sort of religious community. For many, religion offered a source of courage, strength, and hope in the midst of times so bleak that despair seemed the only response. What they received from their religion may be summed up in a story told by Howard Thurman's grandmother, Nancy Ambrose, herself a former slave. She would tell this story to the children, Thurman remembered, whenever it seemed to her that their self-esteem had been damaged by the circumstances of their lives:

> Once or twice a year the master of the plantation allowed a slave preacher from a neighboring plantation to preach to his slaves. The preacher, following an old tradition, would always bring the sermon to its climax by dramatizing the crucifixion and resurrection of Jesus. He would dwell on the agony in the garden of Gethsemane and picture Jesus hanging on the cross; he would recreate Christ's seven last words and the image of his mother Mary standing beneath the cross; he would visualize the sun turning dark and the soldiers struck numb with fear at the empty tomb. By this time the preacher was exhausted but his congregation felt uplifted and restored to face the following week. When the preacher had finished his sermon, he would pause, and stare into every face. Then he would tell them as forcefully as he could: "Remember, you are not niggers! You are not slaves! You are children of God!"

Glossary

Bishop A rank in the ordained Christian ministry. The bishop oversees the affairs of the church in a particular area. Only bishops can ordain others to the ministry.

Bozales Africans who came directly from Africa and were unfamiliar with European culture and religion, did not speak Spanish or Portuguese, and had not received Christian baptism. Literally means "wild" in Spanish.

Camp meeting An extended religious gathering for preaching, praying, and singing. Its purpose is to lead people to the experience of conversion.

Candomblé Afro-Brazilian religion that developed out of the interaction of Portuguese Catholicism with various African religions, especially those of the Yoruba, the Dahomean, and the Kongo peoples.

Conjure See *hoodoo*.

Creole A person of mixed French or Spanish and black descent speaking a dialect of French or Spanish. Creole populations are centered in the Caribbean and United States Gulf states.

Deacon A rank in the ordained Christian ministry. Deacons can preach, and they can distribute communion after the priest or elder has consecrated the bread and wine.

Elder A rank in the Christian ministry. The elder (equivalent to presbyter or priest) can preach and administer the sacraments.

Exhorter A non-ordained layperson who can lead prayer meetings and encourage others to lead a pious Christian life.

Hajj The pilgrimage to Mecca, a religious duty that all Muslims must perform at least once in their lives. Along with daily prayer, giving alms, and fasting, it is one of the tenets of religious life in Islam.

Hoodoo Derived from the word "voodoo," the term refers to magical-medicinal knowledge and practice, often involving the use of roots, herbs, leaves, rituals, and prayers to either heal or harm someone. Also called conjure.

Ladinos Spanish- or Portuguese-speaking Africans who had become familiar with the culture of the Europeans and been baptized into Christianity.

Lwa Haitian creole term for a spirit or god venerated in Vodou.

Orisa Yoruba term for divinity, which is used to refer to the gods in Candomblê and Santería.

Santería Afro-Cuban religion that developed during slavery from the interaction of various African religions and Spanish Catholicism. Santería is practiced widely in the United States because of immigration from Cuba since the 1950s.

Santiago (St. James) An important patron saint for the Spanish and Portuguese, who believed that he helped them reconquer the Iberian peninsula from the Muslims. Therefore, he was called "moor-slayer." The site of his relics (remains) was one of the most important pilgrimage places in Europe. Devotion to Santiago was spread to the Americas and the Philippines by Spanish colonists.

Santos This term refers to African gods who have been identified with Roman Catholic saints in Candomblê and Santería. Literally means "saints" in Spanish.

Vodou An Afro-Haitian religion that developed from the contact between various African religions and French Catholicism. This religion has been brought to the United States by Haitian immigrants. Also spelled vodun and voodoo.

Chronology

1441
Portuguese crusaders capture
Africans off the coast of Mauritania,
beginning the Atlantic slave trade

1496
Ruler of the Kongo converts to
Roman Catholicism; his son, Nzinga
Mvemba, establishes Christianity as
the religion of the court

1502
African slaves brought to Hispaniola;
they are the first to arrive in the
Western Hemisphere

1516
Prince Henrique, the son of Nzinga
Mvemba of the Kongo, is appointed a
bishop of the Roman Catholic
Church; he is consecrated in 1518

1619
About 20 blacks arrive in Jamestown,
Virginia

1664
Maryland legislature passes act denying that baptism entitles slaves to
their freedom

1740
George Whitefield, an English revivalist, tours the American colonies and
reports on large numbers of slaves
attending his revival sermons

1788
Andrew Bryan organizes First African
Church of Savannah

1794
St. Thomas African Episcopal Church
and Bethel African Methodist

Episcopal Church formed in
Philadelphia

1816
African Methodist Episcopal Church
formed in Philadelphia

1821
African Methodist Episcopal Zion
Church established in New York City

1822
Denmark Vesey and members of the
African Methodist Church lead a
slave conspiracy in Charleston, South
Carolina

1829
The Oblate Sisters of Providence, the
first community of African-American
sisters, is approved in Baltimore

1830
First National Negro Convention
meets in Philadelphia with Bishop
Richard Allen as president; Allen dies
within the year

1831
Nat Turner, a slave preacher, organizes the largest slave revolt in the
United States in Southampton, Virginia

1842
The Holy Family Sisters, a religious
community of black women, is organized in New Orleans, Louisiana

1854
James Augustine Healy, the first
African American to become a
Roman Catholic priest, is ordained
in Paris

1870

Colored Methodist Episcopal Church is organized (today it is called the Christian Methodist Episcopal Church)

The Reverend Hiram R. Revels, a black minister, is elected to the U.S. Senate; he is the first African -American senator

1889

The first of five Congresses of Colored Catholics meets; organized by Daniel A. Rudd, a black Catholic journalist

1894

The African Methodist Episcopal Zion Church ordains Julia A. J. Foote as a deacon

1895

The National Baptist Convention of the USA is formed

1900

The National Women's Convention founded as an auxiliary to the National Baptist Convention

1903

W.E.B. DuBois publishes *Souls of Black Folk,* a classic meditation on African-American religion and culture

1906

The Azusa Street Revival in Los Angeles leads to the development of a worldwide Pentecostal movement

1914

Marcus Garvey organizes the Universal Negro Improvement Association and African Communities League

1920

St. Augustine's Seminary is founded in Mississippi to train African Americans for the priesthood

1930

Wallace D. Fard organizes the Nation of Islam movement in Detroit

1933

The National Fraternal Council of Negro Churches is organized to facilitate cooperation among denominations

1955

The Montgomery bus boycott leads to a successful mass protest movement in Alabama

1957

Formation of Southern Christian Leadership Conference, with Martin Luther King, Jr., as president

1963

March on Washington, highlighted by King's "I Have a Dream" speech

1965

Malcolm X assassinated at Audubon Ballroom in New York City

1968

Martin Luther King, Jr., assassinated in Memphis, Tennessee

1975

Elijah Muhammad, leader of the Nation of Islam, dies and is succeeded by his son, Wallace D. Muhammad

1981

Howard Thurman, preacher, poet, mystic, and ecumenist, dies

1987

National Black Catholic Congress meets for the first time in 90 years

1996

The Million Man March, a mass rally of black men to raise issues of family and community responsibility, is held in Washington, D.C.

Further Reading

GENERAL READING ON RELIGION IN THE UNITED STATES

Ahlstrom, Sidney. *A Religious History of the American People.* New Haven, Conn.: Yale University Press, 1972.

Butler, Jon, and Harry S. Stout, eds. *Religion in American History: A Reader.* New York: Oxford University Press, 1997.

Gaustad, Edwin S. *A Religious History of America.* Rev. ed. San Francisco: Harper & Row, 1990.

Marty, Martin. *Pilgrims in Their Own Land: 500 Years of Religion in America.* New York: Penguin, 1985.

AFRICAN-AMERICAN RELIGIOUS FIGURES

Allen, Richard. *The Life Experience and Gospel Labors of the Rt. Rev. Richard Allen.* Nashville: Abingdon, 1960.

Angell, Stephen Ward. *Bishop Henry McNeal Turner and African-American Religion in the South.* Knoxville: University of Tennessee Press, 1992.

Andrews, William L., ed. *Sisters of the Spirit: Three Black Women's Autobiographies of the 19th Century.* Bloomington: Indiana University Press, 1986.

Brown, Karen. *Mama Lola: A Vodou Priestess in Brooklyn.* Berkeley: University of California Press, 1991.

Malcolm X and Alex Haley. *The Autobiography of Malcolm X.* New York: Grove, 1965.

Richardson, Marilyn, ed. *Maria W. Stewart: America's First Black Woman Political Writer.* Bloomington: Indiana University Press, 1987.

Thurman, Howard, *With Head and Heart: The Autobiography of Howard Thurman.* New York: Harcourt Brace Jovanovich, 1979.

Watts, Jill. *God, Harlem, USA: The Father Divine Story.* Berkeley: University of California Press, 1992.

AFRICAN-AMERICAN RELIGIOUS HISTORY

Austin, Allan D. *African Muslims in Antebellum America: Transatlantic Stories and Spiritual Struggles.* New York: Routledge, 1997.

Davis, Cyprian. *The History of Black Catholics in the United States.* New York: Crossroad, 1990.

Davis, Gerald L. *I Got the Word in Me and I Can Sing It, You Know: A Study of the Performed African-American Sermon.* Philadelphia: University of Pennsylvania Press, 1985.

DuBois, W.E.B. *The Souls of Black Folk.* 1903, Reprint, New York: Penguin, 1999.

Fulop, Timothy E., and Albert J. Raboteau. *African-American Religion: Interpretive Essays in History and Culture.* New York: Routledge, 1997.

Garrow, David. *Bearing the Cross: Martin Luther King, Jr., and the Southern Christian Leadership Conference.* New York: Morrow, 1986.

Harris, Michael W. *The Rise of Gospel Blues: The Music of Thomas Andrew Dorsey in the Urban Church.* New York: Oxford University Press, 1992.

Higginbotham, Evelyn Brooks. *Righteous Discontent: The Black Women's Movement in the Black Baptist Church, 1880–1920.* Cambridge, Mass.: Harvard University Press, 1993.

Humez, Jean McMahon, ed. *Gifts of Power: The Writings of Rebecca Cox Jackson, Black Visionary and Shaker Eldress.* Amherst: University of Massachusetts Press, 1981.

Johnson, Clifton H., ed. *God Struck Me Dead: Religious Conversion Experiences and Autobiographies of Ex-Slaves.* Cleveland: Pilgrim Press, 1993.

Johnson, James Weldon. *God's Trombones: Seven Negro Sermons in Verse.* New York: Viking, 1927.

Johnson, Paul E., ed. *African-American Christianity: Essays in History.* Berkeley: University of California Press, 1994.

Lincoln, C. Eric. *The Black Muslims in America.* Boston: Beacon Press, 1961.

———, and Lawrence H. Mamiya. *The Black Church in the African-American Experience.* Durham, N.C.: Duke University Press, 1990.

Raboteau, Albert J. *A Fire in the Bones: Reflections on African-American Religious History.* Boston: Beacon Press, 1995.

———. *Slave Religion: The "Invisible Institution" in the Antebellum South.* New York: Oxford University Press, 1978.

Sernett, Milton C., ed. *Afro-American Religious History: A Documentary Witness.* Durham, N.C.: Duke University Press, 1985.

Washington, James Melvin. *Conversations With God: Two Centuries of Prayers by African-Americans.* New York: HarperCollins, 1994.

———. *Frustrated Fellowship: The Black Baptist Quest for Social Power.* Macon, Ga.: Mercer University Press, 1985.

Weisenfeld, Judith, and Richard Newman, eds. *This Far By Faith: Readings in African-American Women's Religious Biography.* New York: Routledge, 1996.

Wilmore, Gayraud. *Black Religion and Black Radicalism: An Interpretation of the Religious History of Afro-American People.* 2nd ed. Maryknoll, N.Y.: Orbis Books, 1989.

Woodson, Carter G. *The History of the Negro Church.* 3rd ed. Washington, D.C.: Associated Publishers, 1972.

AFRICAN-AMERICAN HISTORY

Branch, Taylor. *Parting the Waters: America in the King Years, 1954–1963.* New York: Simon & Schuster, 1988.

———. *Pillar of Fire: America in the King Years, 1963–1965.* Simon & Schuster, 1998.

Genovese, Eugene. *Roll, Jordan, Roll: The World the Slaves Made.* New York: Vintage, 1972.

Sobel, Mechal. *The World They Made Together: Black and White Values in 18th-Century Virginia.* Princeton, N.J.: Princeton University Press, 1987.

Thompson, Robert Farris. *Flash of the Spirit: African and Afro-American Art and Philosophy.* New York: Vintage, 1983.

Thornton, John. *Africa and Africans in the Making of the Atlantic World, 1400–1680.* Cambridge: Cambridge University Press, 1992.

Index

Acknowledgments

This slim volume represents the synthesis of a great deal of historical work accomplished over the last three decades by many scholars. I wish to acknowledge several whose scholarship and friendship have informed and encouraged me: Randall Burkett, Will B. Gravely, the late James M. Washington, and David W. Wills. I also am grateful to several generations of undergraduate and graduate students whose thoughtful questions have constantly challenged me to think more deeply and write more clearly about the history of African American Religion. My wife, Julia Demaree, and the regular members of the writing workshop of the Souls in Motion Studio in Harlem (James, Ethel, Cordelia, Gibbons, Lorna, Vernel, Maxine, and Patricia) offer me loving support and precious community during the lonely periods of writing. Thank you. Finally, to my children, Albert, Emily, Charles, and Martin, I offer this book with a father's love. May the strength, wisdom, and compassion of the religious heritage I've attempted to describe be yours and your children's.

Picture Credits

Albert J. Raboteau

Albert J. Raboteau is the Henry W. Putnam Professor of Religion at Princeton University. He is the author of *Slave Rebellion: The "Invisible Institution" in the Antebellum South* which won the African Roots Award of the African Studies Association in 1978. He also has written *A Fire in the Bones: Reflection on African-American Religious History* and is co-editor of a multi-volume series, "African-American Religion: An Historical Interpretation with Representative Documents."

Jon Butler

Jon Butler is the William Robertson Coe Professor of American Studies and History and Professor of Religious Studies at Yale University. He received his B.A. and Ph.D. in history from the University of Minnesota. He is the coauthor, with Harry S. Stout, of *Religion in American History: A Reader*, and the author of several other books on American religious history including *Awash in a Sea of Faith: Christianizing the American People*, which won the Beveridge Award for the best book in American history in 1990 from the American Historical Association.

Harry S. Stout

Harry S. Stout is the Jonathan Edwards Professor of American Christianity at Yale University. He is the general editor of the Religion in America series for Oxford University Press and co-editor of *Readings in American Religious History*, *New Directions in American Religious History*, *A Jonathan Edwards Reader*, and *The Dictionary of Christianity in America*. His book *The Divine Dramatist: George Whitefield and the Rise of Modern Evangelicalism* was nominated for a Pulitzer Prize in 1991.